MW01127405

THE ORIGINS CONTROVERSY: CREATION BY DESIGN OR CHANCE

VOLUME III
CREATION SCIENCE SERIES

By Dennis Gordon Lindsay

Published by
Christ For The Nations Inc.
P.O. Box 769000
Dallas, TX 75376-9000

First Printing 1991
Second Printing 2007
Copyright © 1991 by
Christ For The Nations Inc.

Cover design by Don Day.
Illustrations by:
Wayne Johnson, Diana Sisco, Camille Barnes and Carlos Cazarez.

TABLE OF CONTENTS

Introduction

Why is man trying to unlock the secrets of the universe? Why is the U.S. government spending billions of dollars on space research and exploration? Why was a 1.5 billion-dollar telescope, placed in orbit in April of 1990? Why was this achievement considered the biggest advancement in astronomy since Galileo's work in the 1600s? Will this new space telescope be able to stare back to the very origin of time as is reported in *U.S. News and World Report*, March 26, 1990? The answer is simple. Man is seeking to discover his origins. One of the most popular computer software programs is for designing a family tree. Everyone wants to know where they came from.

Why did the U.S. plan to spend over six billion dollars to construct an atom smasher in the heart of Texas? Can mankind ever understand the nature of matter and how it all originated? What is the universe made of and what force binds its parts together? Why are the experimentalists we are told about in the April 16, 1990 edition of *Time* magazine creating tiny fireballs 400 million times as hot as the sun?

When was the universe new? What is the truth about creation? How did it begin? How can the biblical explanation stack up against 21st century science? Have laboratory experiments revealed that life could have risen spontaneously by chance if given enough time and the right combination of chemicals and conditions?

The Book of Genesis is often regarded, by cynical evolutionists, as nothing but a collection of myths and legends from primitive societies. Some believe the stories to be allegories, with certain moral and spiritual values, though not true in a literal, historical sense. What is the truth about the origin of the universe, Earth and life? Did all of the world's plants and animals grow out of a glob of primordial slime?

In the United States, only 30 percent of the young people brought up in the Church succeed at having an active faith when they become adults. In other words, the Church is losing 70 percent of its young people. Why? If you can't get a young person to believe the first chapter of Genesis, then it follows you will have a difficult time getting them to believe John 3:16. Within five minutes of witnessing to college age students the issue of evolutionism comes up in conversation. Yet the Church, by and large, has looked at the evolutionism controversy as a fringe issue rather than a foundational issue.

Students are taught in high school that people "share a common heritage with earthworms"[i] and that "evolution is random and undirected … without either plan or purpose ... "[ii] Isn't it interesting that today's generation of young people seem to have the same tendencies? Should we be surprised when teens live out what they are being taught? In *Scientific American* we read, "Yes, we are all animals, descendants of a vast lineage of replicators sprung from primordial pond scum."[iii]

> When the foundations are being destroyed, what can the righteous do? (Psa.11:3).

Without a biblical foundation for learning about creation there will be little understanding of the need of a Creator and even less of an understanding of the need for a Savior. A biblical view of creation is essential for a young person to grow and appreciate the Creator and to learn to worship Him. Creation Science equips the believer with tools to demolish arguments. II Corinthians 10:5 instructs the believer to demolish arguments against God's Word. As we consider Scripture, we shall see that all true scientific and historical evidence does, in fact, support the truth of the biblical record. Furthermore, it will become plain that the purposes of God in His majestic plan of salvation are inseparably bound to these same events.

The doctrine of creation is the central doctrine of Scripture. The Bible begins with "In the beginning God created ..." (Gen. 1:1). Thus the first written record of God chronicles the act of creation, giving it a preeminent place in Scripture. Viewing creation as the central and foremost doctrine of Scripture does not in any way detract from the value, meaning, purpose or place of Christ. This is because the creationist worldview recognizes Jesus Christ as the Creator (Jn. 1:1-3; Col. 1:16). In fact, an argument could be made that there would be no need for a Savior if there were no act of creation. Opposing evolutionary worldview advocates have often made such a claim, stating that there is no God and that everything has its origins in some naturalistic process, thus negating the need for Jesus Christ. For example, evolutionist Richard Bozarth stated:

> Christianity has fought, still fights, and will fight science to the desperate end of evolution, because evolution destroys utterly and finally the very reason Jesus' earthly life was supposedly made necessary. Destroy Adam and Eve and the original sin, and in the rubble you will find the sorry remains of the Son of God. Take away the meaning of His death. If Jesus was not the Redeemer who died for our sins, and this is what evolution means, then Christianity is nothing.[iv]

Mr. Bozarth clearly understands that to destroy the Creator will result in there being no need for a Savior. Charles Darwin wanted to replace the Creator with a naturalistic mechanism in order to avoid any responsibility.

CHAPTER ONE

Creation Myths of the Past

Dumb on Purpose

> For this they willingly are ignorant of, that by the
> word of God the heavens were of old, and the earth
> standing out of the water and in the water (II Pet.
> 3:5 KJV).

Peter tells us that people are willfully ignorant. In
other words they chose to be dumb on purpose. People
deliberately deny the faith.

> Since what may be known about God is plain to
> them, because God has made it plain to them.
> For since the creation of the world God's invisible
> qualities — his eternal power and divine nature
> — have been clearly seen, being understood from
> what has been made, so that men are without
> excuse. For although they knew God, they neither
> glorified him as God nor gave thanks to him, but
> their thinking became futile and their foolish hearts
> were darkened. Although they claimed to be wise,
> they became fools and exchanged the glory of the
> immortal God for images made to look like mortal
> man and birds and animals and reptiles. Therefore

God gave them over in the sinful desires of their hearts to sexual impurity for the degrading of their bodies with one another. They exchanged the truth of God for a lie, and worshiped and served created things rather than the Creator — who is forever praised. Amen (Rom. 1:19-25).

Have you heard the many accounts of various traditions and religions from around the world about how creation took place? They are filled with fantastic and ridiculous beliefs. Greek mythology, for instance, pictures Atlas balancing a celestial globe on his shoulder. **(See fig. #1)**. When people deliberately deny the faith, they begin to think up silly ideas about where they came from. On the other hand, the Bible reveals a story of creation that closely harmonizes with the latest scientific discoveries (not theories) regarding the origins of the universe.

Ignorance and Superstition

During the period in which the Old Testament was written, ignorance, superstition and foolishness dominated the minds of ungodly men. The Babylonians believed Earth came about as a result of a battle between two giant gods: Marduk rolled up Tiamu into a ball and tied his tail to his nose. This ball became Earth. When Marduk spit, a man grew, and when man spit, an animal grew. This was actually considered to be fact. What an exciting concept — all life was made from slobber!

The absence of scientific error in the Word of God

Figure 1: *Atlas balancing the earth on his shoulders*

Throughout mankind's history, many fantastic and ridiculous creation accounts have surfaced. Greek mythology, for instance, pictures Atlas balancing a celestial globe upon his shoulders

is astounding, especially as one studies other ancient writings and sees the obvious scientific blunders. In the sacred writings of the Hindus, for instance, one finds such erroneous, even ridiculous, statements as the moon is 50,000 leagues (10,000 miles) higher than the sun and shines by its own light; Earth is flat and rectangular and is composed of seven layers: one of honey, another of sugar, a third of butter, another of wine, and so forth. **(See fig. #2.)** In the Koran, the sacred book of the Muslims, the stars are said to be torches set in the lower heavens and men are made out of baked clay.

The account in the Koran is similar to another creation myth telling how the various skin colors of man came to be. It seems God was inexperienced when

Figure 2: An ancient concept of the Earth's composition

The further man became removed from the Garden and God's presence, the more his understanding became darkened. Absurd beliefs emerged, such as a Hindu legend that the Earth is composed of seven layers: one of honey, one of sugar, a third of butter, another of wine ...

He created man. He first fashioned man from clay, then placed the figure into His kiln. After some time He withdrew man, but He came out black. So God tried a second time, cutting the baking time in half. This time the creature came out white. Finally, God set his timer between the previous two settings and the creature came out nice and brown.

Egg Foo Creation

An ancient Chinese version of creation reveals another incredulous account:

In the beginning, the heavens and Earth were still one and all was chaos. The universe was like a big, black egg, with Pan Gu being carried inside. After 18,000 years, Pan Gu woke from a long sleep. He felt suffocated, so he took a broadax and wielded it with all his might to crack open the egg. The light, clear part of the egg floated up and formed the heavens. The cold, turbid matter stayed below to form Earth. The heavens and the Earth began to grow at a rate of 10 feet per day, and Pan Gu grew along with them. After another 18,000 years, the sky was higher and the Earth thicker. Pan Gu stood between them like a pillar nine million li in height, so heaven and Earth would never join again.

When Pan Gu died, his breath became the wind and clouds, his voice the rolling thunder. One eye became the sun and one became the moon. His body and limbs turned to five big mountains and his blood formed the roaring water. His veins became far-stretching roads and his muscles fertile land. The innumerable stars in the sky came from his hair and beard, and flowers and trees from his skin and the fine hairs on his body. His marrow turned to jade and pearls. His sweat flowed like the good rain and sweet dew that nurtured all things on Earth. According to some versions of the Pan Gu legend, his tears flowed to make the rivers and the radiance of his eyes turned into thunder and lightning. When he was happy the sun shone, but when he was angry, black clouds gathered in the sky. One version of the legend has it that the fleas and lice on his body became the ancestors of mankind.

Today, we find the foolishness of these accounts humorous, but they depict the element of error that persists in creation accounts among the ancient religious traditions of people worldwide. Historical research has revealed that as man departed from the truth, his views about God and His creation became distorted.

Anything ancient mankind couldn't understand was attributed to supernatural powers. Eventually people began to worship these unexplainable events, objects and phenomena. As a result, perverted concepts about the creation of the universe and life developed among the pagan tribes and civilizations, even to the point of including demonic activities, such as religious sexual rites and human sacrifices. This is what Paul was speaking of in Romans chapter one.

The Word *Bara*

Scripture, however, shares a plausible account of creation:

In the beginning God created the heavens and the earth (Gen.1:1 NAS).

The Hebrew word *bara*, which was used in Genesis 1:1 is translated to English as "created." It means "to call

into being something that never previously existed."
God simply spoke, and *nothing* became *something*. A
helpful example that provides a partial understanding of
God's creative abilities is computer voice recognition. I
occasionally use a program on my computer that allows
me to speak directly to my computer, and the computer
automatically types out my words and commands. In fact,
it will type as rapidly as I can speak. It can even correct
my grammar mistakes automatically. If a word has several
spellings, the computer will ask me which spelling I
prefer. All of this is accomplished without my touching
the computer. It even recognizes my Texas accent. As
amazing as this is, God has the ability to speak things into
existence.

Some theologians who have a difficult time accepting
the Genesis account of Creation in such a short span of
time have suggested that God incorporated evolutionism
as part of His method of Creation. This is known as
theistic evolutionism. However, why would God use such
a method? That would be such a wasteful, inefficient,
non-powerful, non-indicative way for God to create. My
Bible states that He spoke and instantly it was.

Again in verse 21, God uses *bara* to indicate that the
animal world was another distinct, creative act of God. He
brought the animals into being out of that which never
previously existed. There is absolutely no room here for
evolutionism, with its supposedly-new species evolving
from already existing species. *Bara* means "created out of

no existing matter." The first verse of the Bible is the most important and basic verse of the *entire* Bible. When one really believes this verse, he/she will have little difficulty believing the rest of God's Word. This verse refutes the doctrine of atheism, the disbelief in God, because it begins with God. It also refutes the concept of pantheism (the belief that nature is God) because it shows that God existed *before* the universe.

More Mystifying Myths

When compared to the creation story in Genesis, it becomes apparent that the beliefs of the Hindus, Buddhists, Muslims and others are based on absurd theories. In the sacred books of the Hindus, we read about how millions upon millions of cycles ago, this world came to be. The world is several stories in height, and the whole mass is held on the heads of elephants, standing with their tails turned out and their feet resting on the shell of an immense tortoise. The tortoise is on the coil of a snake, and when the elephants shake themselves, the Earth quakes. **(See fig. #3.)**

Japanese Creation Myth

Long ago all the elements were mixed together with one germ of life. This germ began to mix things around and around until the heavier part sank and the lighter part rose. A muddy sea that covered the entire Earth was created. From this ocean grew a green shoot. It grew and grew until it reached the clouds, and there it was

Figure 3: A Hindu belief regarding the way the earth is held

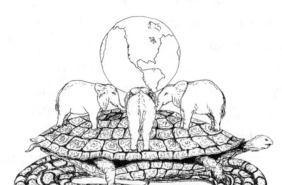

An ancient Hindu account suggests that the earth rests on the back of four elephants, which stand on the back of a giant turtle, which rests on the back of a coiled snake.

transformed into a god. Soon this god grew lonely and began to create other gods. The last two gods it made, Izanagi and Izanami, were the most remarkable.

One day, as they were walking along, they looked down on the ocean and wondered what was beneath it. Izanagi thrust his staff into the waters and as he pulled it back up, some clumps of mud fell back into the sea. They began to harden and grow until they became the islands of Japan.

The two gods descended to these islands and began to explore, each going in different directions. They created all kinds of plants. When they met again, they decided to marry and have children to inhabit the land. The first child Izanami bore was a girl of radiant beauty. The gods decided she was too beautiful to live in Japan, so they put her up in the sky and she became the sun. Their second daughter, Tsuki-yami, became the moon and their third, an unruly son, Sosanowo, was sentenced to the sea, where he creates storms. Later, their first child, Amaterasu, bore a son who became the emperor of Japan and all the emperors since then have claimed their descent from him.

One spiritual master of the Hare Krishna movement gives this unearthly account of creation:

The spiritual godhead or Krishna (sometimes they are one and the same) goes and sits (we are not told where) with all four arms extended and eyes shut and begins to meditate. As he does this, gold beads begin to sweat out of the pores of his skin and float in the air around him. Then the four-armed god opens his eyes and looks at the beads. By doing this, he fills all the beads with billions of souls. Each gold bead becomes a universe. Then the gold will lie down in consciousness, like one would lie down in a puddle of water. When this is done, a lotus flower sprouts out of his navel, and the universe will spiral around the stem of the flower to its base. As the universe does this, the god creates demi-gods, who then create the matter (bodies) which will encase the souls. Every living thing has a soul: every blade of grass, every tree, animal and human.

The Chinese tell us their god, Pwangu, carved the heavens out of granite. Thales of Miletus (600 B.C.) taught that water was the origin of all things. Heraclituss of Ephesus (500 B.C.) held that fire was the origin of everything. In Moses' day, the Egyptians led the world in science, yet their best scholars taught, as Plato informs us, that both Earth and the heavens originated out of a kind of pulp, and men were generated from the slime of the River Nile. Other Egyptian sages taught that Earth was hatched from a winged egg.

Today, all of these conjectures regarding the conception of the universe are considered laughable. On the other hand, the teachings in Genesis remarkably agree with the greatest scientific findings of the past 50 years. These discoveries reveal the universe had a sharply defined beginning — it commenced at a certain moment in time.

> In the beginning was the Word, and the Word was with God, and the Word was God. He was with God in the beginning. Through him all things were made; without him nothing was made that has been made (Jn. 1:1-3).

CHAPTER TWO

The Battle Over Origins

Which Came First, the Chicken or the Egg?

For decades this question has been a standing joke to humanity's ignorance of the creation order.

> For although they knew God, they neither glorified him as God nor gave thanks to him, but their thinking became futile and their foolish hearts were darkened (Rom. 1:21).

Figure 4: Which came first, the chicken or the egg?

God created everything in a mature state; the chicken came first.

The answer to this riddle, of course, is neither; God was first. **(See fig. #4.)** However, according to the doctrine of mature creation, the answer to the fowl stumper would be the adult chicken. But in fact, long before the chicken was created, wisdom existed.

> By wisdom the Lord laid the earth's foundations ... (Prov. 3:19).

It is the fear of the Lord which is the beginning or wisdom (Psa. 111:10), but fools despise wisdom (Prov. 1:7). Therefore they despise God's Word which proclaims, "In the beginning God created the heavens and the earth" (Gen 1:1).

Genesis: The Book of Beginnings

The word *genesis* is a Greek word meaning "origin." The Book of Genesis sets forth the beginning of the heavens and the Earth; the beginning of man and of sin; the beginning of salvation and of punishment. Genesis is the seed-plot of the Bible. Almost every Christian doctrine of major importance has its roots in this book.

Genesis is quoted, or alluded to, more than 200 times in the New Testament and half of those refer to the first 11 chapters of Genesis. Jesus obviously accepted the Book of Genesis as historically trustworthy, as well as divinely inspired. He quoted from it and never once did He indicate anything in it was unreliable.

Some of the sharpest attacks on the Bible have been directed against the first 11 chapters of Genesis. Satan knows the quickest way to demolish a building is to strike at its foundation. If a person can be persuaded to pull out the first pages of the Bible, the last pages will fall out too, and soon not much will be left.

A College Memory

I still have a vivid memory of a classroom encounter in which my Christian faith was attacked during my freshman year at a state university. The professor asked if there was anyone in the class who still believed the Genesis account of creation. Only one other person lifted his hand, and I was too embarrassed to lift mine above my shoulder. The instructor responded sarcastically, "You're kidding," made a couple of derogatory remarks and continued teaching. This took place back in the middle 1960s. Today, professors are much more blatant and vocal in their attacks against Christianity.

At that time, I was not equipped with the necessary tools to withstand such a humanistic attack against my faith in God and His Word. Thank God, today the believer — young or old — has access to plenty of good Christian apologetic material. Ample evidence with which to stand against any such anti-God forces of the enemy may be found.

Christian parents and church leaders must explain the dangers of evolutionism and expose the deceptive nature of the theory. The science books used in the public school systems today are undermining the

Bible's authority. Children's textbooks are professionally packaged to influence young, impressionable minds to question the reliability of the biblical story of creation.

For example, I recently purchased an attractively published book entitled *Eyewitness Science-Evolutionism.* The book is beautifully illustrated so children will enjoy its contents. On the very first page, it shares stories about creation from different religions around the world. The first story is taken from the Bible. The text actually states that the Bible has two versions of the creation story. The book explains that in the first story, man and woman are created together. In the second story, man is created first and the woman came later and still later, the animals were created.

So what has the book done? It has deceptively interpreted the first two chapters of Genesis to read as though the Bible contains two different versions of creation. This misrepresentation of the biblical story of creation was mixed in with other absurd, unscientific accounts of creation from several other world religions. Seeds of doubt regarding the Bible's accuracy are planted in the mind of any child reading this book. Evolutionary authors have a hidden agenda: to dissuade students regarding any religious beliefs they have been taught.

The creative events of the first two chapters of Genesis may be more clearly understood by considering verse one of chapter one as a summary statement that describes the relative beginning of everything, without any reference

to specifics except the creation of time, space and matter.
The picture of creation presented in Genesis 2:4-25
compliments the events recorded in chapter one, which
portray with broad strokes the creation of heaven and
Earth and, rather generally, the contents of the universe.
Chapter two then uses finer strokes to paint the specific
features. This section describes the Garden of Eden with
geographical detail, even noting the names of the rivers.
It depicts the creation of the first human couple, their
ideal garden surroundings and the intimacy of their
relationship.

While the creation of man is the climax of chapter
one, it serves as the centerpiece of chapter two. The love
and tender care of God are apparent in the creation of the
Garden of Eden. He meticulously prepared everything
else in creation first as the ideal home for man. God's
gentle, divine breath brought life to the lifeless clay figure
of Adam. The relationship between God and this innocent
first couple was one of great intimacy. Adam and Eve were
surrounded with God's love. Yet even here, the divine
command clearly reveals the possibility of disobedience
and broken relationship.

Mankind's dignity and unique position in creation
are marked by the image of God. Again, biblical truth
aggressively attacked the prevailingly doctrines of that
day. Other ancient Near Eastern creation accounts, such
as the *Enuma Elish* and the Atrahasis epic portray the
creation of men and women as a slave force for the gods.

Humanity was more or less a means for the gods to avoid physical labor. But in Genesis one, humankind is the jewel in this literary crown, the climax of God's creative activity.

Genesis portrays God as the divine artist who stands back to admire his handiwork. Man was free to serve Him in complete obedience. When the chapter states, "These are the generations ..." it is another way of saying, "This is the history ..."

Understanding Evolutionism is Critical

It is crucial that we understand today's evolutionary point of view, which is infected with deceptive philosophies. Christians have often been afraid to examine the subject of evolutionism, and it is true there are certain areas of knowledge forbidden by God to man. However, a study of the evolutionary theory can be advantageous, especially to the mature believer. We must be aware of Satan's clever strategies of deception, and evolutionism is high on the list. An examination of evolutionism will not only reveal that it is based on a very shaky foundation, but it will also reveal the real debate: Whether or not there is a God.

Ignorance is Not Always Bliss

The scientific-thinking person, finding there is conflict between the evolutionary theory he has been taught and what the Bible teaches, has a definite need to have his questions resolved. Christians often put on "spiritual blinders" when it comes to the evolutionism question, and simply respond, "God created the universe; the Bible says it; that settles it." But such an attitude isn't of much help to one truly struggling with the harmony between science and Scripture.

Children who grow up in a home where the creation/ evolutionism issue is avoided altogether will have a very difficult time if they go to a college where evolutionism is taught. Many will feel pressure from professors and peers who taunt that "not believing in evolutionism is like not believing in gravity."

What Difference Does it Make?

A person's view of his or her origin and the origins of life affects his or her whole outlook on life. At some point in life, everyone deals with questions such as: Who am I? Where did I come from? Does my life have meaning? Am I of any value?

What people believe about their origin will determine what they believe about themselves and their place in life. If they think they are merely complex animals that evolved from one-celled creatures instead of unique individuals made in the image of God with eternal destinies, then existence has no meaning. Why not eat, drink and enjoy all the world has to offer, for tomorrow comes death? God has created each person to reveal an aspect of His infinite love and character, which no one else — past, present or future — can reveal. Each one of us is unique; there are no duplicates. Knowledge of this fact makes life worth living. Settling this matter regarding the creation of the universe, the Earth and life is critical. Many facets of life are impacted by the decision people make concerning the Creator and their origins. Harold Hill aptly expressed this in his book *From Goo to You by Way of the Zoo*:

> In the beginning — what? Evolution says — Goo. The Bible says — God. Does evolution really provide the answer? Did we actually descend from freak apes? Were our beginnings in a sea of chemical soup? Or in a cloud of hot gases? And if so, where did the soup of gases come from? Or is it just possible that a Supreme Being — God Himself — carefully engineered and created the whole show?

CHAPTER THREE

In the Beginning: How, When and Why?

> For in six days the LORD made the heavens and the
> earth, the sea, and all that is in them, but he rested
> on the seventh day. Therefore the LORD blessed the
> Sabbath day and made it holy (Ex. 20:11).

Creationists and evolutionists are diametrically
opposed regarding the origin of life and the origin of
life forms. Basically, the controversy boils down to this:
Creationists believe there is a supernatural explanation or
cause behind the universe, while the evolutionists believe
it all came about by chance. The controversy concerns
whether the cause of the universe is intelligent or non-
intelligent. The whole issue boils down to this question:
"Can God exist?"

The controversy between evolutionists isn't over
evidence, rather it is about God the Creator. This is clearly
revealed by Richard Lewontin, an eminent Harvard
biologist, when he states that he will always choose a
naturalistic explanation in such a situation:

> We take the side of science in spite of the patent
> absurdity of some of its constructs, in spite of its

failure to fulfill many of its extravagant promises of health and life, in spite of the tolerance of the scientific community for unsubstantiated, just so stories, because we have a prior commitment, a commitment to materialism. It is not that the methods and institutions of science somehow compel us to accept a material explanation of the phenomenal world, but, on the contrary, that we are first by our a priori adherence to material causes to create and apparatus of investigation and a set of concepts that produce material explanations, no matter how counterintuitive, no matter how mystifying to uninitiated. Moreover, that materialism is absolute, for we cannot allow a divine fluid in the door.[v]

Or, in other words, "Our faith in materialism is absolute, for we cannot allow any thought of a Divine Creator in our thoughts, discussions or ideas in any way, fashion or manner now and forever."

Figure 5: Ptolemy's conception of an earth-centered universe

Second Law of Thermodynamics Confirms a Beginning

The universe can be shown to have had a beginning, as even one of the most basic and fundamental laws of physics, the second law of thermodynamics, testifies. The second law states, in effect, that the universe must have had a beginning. Otherwise, since it is now running down like a battery that can't be recharged, it would already be dead.[1] And anything having a beginning had to have a cause.

The first law of thermodynamics (equally as important as the second law) states that the universe could not have created itself. Therefore, it must have been created by some greater cause beyond itself. This principle is clear and undeniable, yet some evolutionists dispute it. Only a person who has a religious, humanistic bias would be able to do so, since there is absolutely no evidence for such thinking. Based on the known laws of science, "In the beginning God created the heavens and the earth," is the most scientific statement that could possibly be made about the origins of the universe.

When Did It All Begin?

Nowhere does Scripture say exactly how old the creation is. Calculations, using the genealogies listed in the Bible, point to an approximate age of 6,000 years. If the seven days of the creation week described in Genesis chapter one are accepted as literal 24-hour days, then

---

1   The second law of thermodynamics is discussed in Volume II and is also discussed in chapter ten of this volume.

all of creation — the entire universe — is approximately 6,000 years old.

Literal "Days" of Creation

Following Scripture's own rules for usage, the word "day" in Genesis cannot mean anything other than a literal, 24-hour day. For instance, if we were to say, "In George Washington's day, there were no airplanes," we would be referring to a point in time covering many years. But when we say, "Wednesday is the fourth day of the week," we are referring to a 24-hour day. Whenever a number is associated with the word "day," this signifies a 24-hour day. This association is what we find in the creation account of Genesis chapter one.

To many, the idea of such a recent creation is unbelievable. It is true that the concept is incredible, especially in the light of the evolutionary dogma we have been taught regarding the age of the universe. However, in the realm of origin theories, the alternatives are absurd. The dominant evolutionary scenario for the beginning, the Big Bang theory, is certainly a ridiculous notion.

Since no one was present to substantiate what happened in the beginning, the choice one makes regarding this matter is determined solely on the basis of one's faith: faith in God or faith in matter. This issue is not really how or when creation took place, but whether or not God truly exists.

Figure 6: The evolutionary concept of how a solar system is formed

The evolutionary concept says planets evolve from a cloud of gases. This theory is filled with hundreds of abnormalities, inconsistencies and contradictions which totally discredit it.

How Did It All Begin?

Most cosmologists (scientists who study the structure and origins of the universe) agree with the biblical assertion that the universe began at a specific point in time. Even the evolutionists agree on this; however, rather than accrediting God as the Creator, they believe the universe is the result of an expanding remnant of a huge fireball created 20 billion years ago by the explosion of a "prehistoric primordial embryonic atom," whatever that is. **(See fig. #6.)**

When considering the difference in the age theories of the *universe* between the young-earth creation position and the ancient evolutionary concept of 20 to 30 billion years (depending on which evolutionistic source you refer to) — which includes assigning an age of 4 ½ billion years to the *Earth* — we are considering a number that is hard to visualize. Imagine a book where each page represents one year — to depict the evolutionary age of the universe at 20 billion years would require a stack of books 450 miles high, while the biblical view of the Earth's age at 6,000 years would have a stack of books only knee high. Of course, the heart and blood of evolutionism is time, without which evolutionism is dead.

To explain the origin of our solar system alone, at least 23 different evolutionary theories have been concocted. And no doubt more will be forthcoming, since not one of them fits the observable data — especially that which strongly suggests a Designer. If there are 23

Figure 7: The Big Bang Theory (Cosmic Egg Theory)

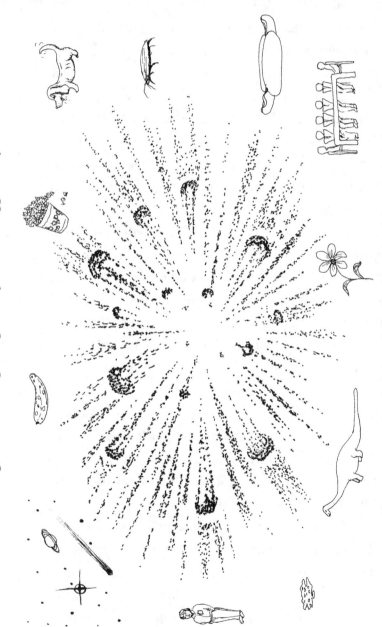

The most accepted evolutionary theory for the origin of the universe is the Big Bang Theory, also known as the Cosmic Egg theory.

theories regarding the origin of our sun and its nine planets, imagine how many theories there must be among evolutionists regarding the origin of the entire universe!

The Cosmic Egg Theory: Hydrogen to Humans

The most accepted theory among evolutionists for the origin of the universe is the Cosmic Egg theory, or the Big Bang theory. According to the evolutionary scenario, all the matter of the universe was once in a tiny ball, perhaps the size of the head of a pin. This object sat in space for some unspecified period of time. Then suddenly, for no reason at all, the tiny ball became unstable, exploded and eventually turned into stars, planets, pickles, popcorn, puppy dogs, corny dogs, cockroaches, committees, daffodils, dinosaurs, primordial embryonic goo and you. **(See fig. #7.)** In other words: Nothing + no one = everything with no purpose.

Building on this theory, evolutionists have envisioned a still-expanding universe, which not only began almost 20 billion years ago, but also extends for 20 billion light years and contains as many as 100 billion galaxies — each one an island of hundreds of billions of stars.

Can Explosions Create Order?

Though "scientific" articles repeatedly refer to the Big Bang as a reasonable explanation for the origin of the universe, the physical realities in the heavens, as well as on Earth, defy the possibility of such an explosion being responsible for the present state of the universe. The

*Figure 8: Mount St. Helens after
the 1980 eruption*

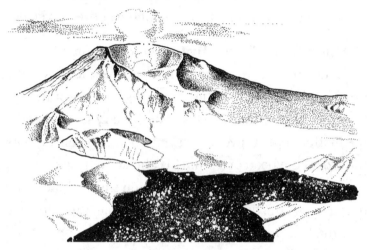

*In 1980, when Mount St. Helens (northwestern U.S.) blew up with a
blast equal to many times the force of a nuclear bomb, everything for
miles around was desolated; the area was labeled a "dead zone."*

biggest problem with the theory is that nowhere in the universe have ordered arrangements been produced due to an explosion; in fact, the opposite is true — explosions inevitably create disorder.

In 1980, when Mount St. Helens, in the northwestern U.S., blew up with a blast equal to many times the force of a nuclear bomb explosion, everything for miles around was desolated; the area was called a "dead zone." **(See fig. #8.)** No orderliness whatsoever resulted from that explosion, nor has any explosion ever resulted in anything other than chaos and destruction. Yet, evolutionists tell us that the original "big bang" explosion somehow managed to produce order rather than disorder. In other words, evolutionism claims if you shake a box of Lego pieces, you will get something like an airplane that a child can put together and it will have symmetrical wings, hinged doors and a rotating prop. Evolutionism is simply a fairy tale for adults.

Abnormalities in Our Solar System Discredit the Big Bang Theory

If the Big Bang theory were true and an explosion could cause order, the planets should all rotate in the same direction on their axes; but Venus and Uranus both rotate differently from the other planets. The several dozen moons of our solar system should all orbit their respective planets in the same direction, but at least a dozen of them orbit in the opposite direction from the rest. The orbits of all the moons would be expected to lie flat over the equatorial planes; however, a number of the moons follow a highly tilted orbit.

To account for the discrepancies in their theory, evolutionists claim random accidents occurred. But how can they explain the fact that planets are formed of different materials? The outer planets are made of lighter weight materials than the inner planets. And the atmospheres of each of the planets differ sharply. The differences are far too numerous and the variations much too obvious to allow credibility to the Big Bang theory. **(See Fig. #9.)**

Figure 9: Abnormalities within our solar system

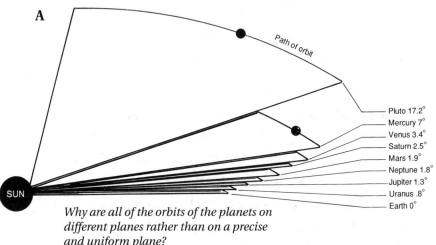

Why are all of the orbits of the planets on different planes rather than on a precise and uniform plane?

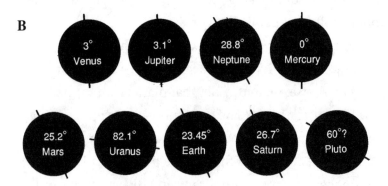

Why is there such diversity among the planets as to their axis angle?

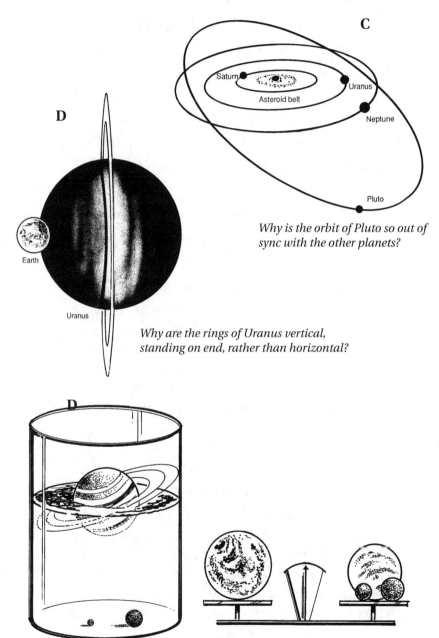

C

Why is the orbit of Pluto so out of sync with the other planets?

Why are the rings of Uranus vertical, standing on end, rather than horizontal?

Why are the planets formed of different materials?

The space program has provided proof that every planet, and the moons of each, differ radically. More discrepancies in the Big Bang theory are continually being discovered as space probes send back photographs and technical data from their journeys into the far reaches of our solar system. Most likely, the Big Bang theory will eventually have to be discarded in light of the evidences against it.

On the basis of so many recent observations being contrary to what was expected, science writer John Maddox comments:

> … It is exceedingly improbable that the succeeding decade will allow the persistence of present views of how the universe is constructed. The Big Bang itself is the pinnacle of a chain of inference which provides no explanation at present for quasars and the source of the known hidden mass in the universe. It will be a surprise if it somehow survives the Hubble telescope.[vi]

Likewise, astronomer Fred Hoyle writes:

> As a result of all this the main efforts of investigators have been in papering over holes in the Big Bang theory, to build up an idea that has become ever more complex and cumbersome. … I have little hesitation in saying that a sickly pall now hangs over the Big Bang theory. When a pattern of facts becomes set against a theory, experience shows that the theory rarely recovers.[vii]

Humanistic scientists are learning that many of their most cherished theories of Earth's origins must be revised. Dr. Murray, former director of the Jet Propulsion laboratory in Pasadena and the architect of many of this country's planetary missions, states, "The whole concept of the early history of the Earth is being revised."

The Entire Universe Operates According to Precise Laws

Observation reveals our universe and everything in it operates according to precise laws, functioning in an orderly manner. And disorder in the universe can be traced to once-orderly systems that are breaking apart and decaying. Only a creative God could have produced both the order and the variety seen in the universe. The disorder came as a result of the curse pronounced upon Adam and Eve by God as a consequence of their rebellion.

The Biblical Account of Creation

The basic elements of the astronomical account and the biblical account of the origins of the universe are essentially the same: Creation took place at a definite moment in time with a tremendous flash of energy.

> The crux of the new story of Genesis, better known as the "Big Bang" theory, is that we live in an expanding universe in which all the galaxies around us are moving away from us and one another at enormous speeds. ... It is as if we are witnessing the aftermath of a gigantic explosion. If we trace the motions of the outward-moving

galaxies backward in time, we find that they all come together. ...[viii]

The above excerpt from a *Reader's Digest* article accurately depicts that the universe's beginning resulted from an enormous amount of energy. The main difference between those who believe in the biblical view of creation and advocates of the Big Bang theory is the source of power behind the creation of the universe. The evolutionists assert that a non-intelligent source is responsible, whereas creationists maintain an intelligent source is responsible.

Agnostic Robert Jastrow, in his book *God and the Astronomers*, admits the astronomical evidence leads to a biblical view of the origin of the universe. Jastrow is the founder and director of the Goddard Institute for Space and is one of the leading astrophysicists in the U.S.

Yes, the most reasonable explanation for the origin of the universe is, "In the beginning God ..."

CHAPTER FOUR

Building Blocks of Creation

In the beginning God created the heavens and the earth. ... And God said, 'Let there be light,' and there was light (Gen. 1:1, 3).

What does the Bible have to offer the scientific mind of the 21st century regarding the universe and the building blocks necessary for its construction? Right in the first three verses of the first chapter of the first book of the Bible we find the building blocks of creation. **(See fig. #10.)**

When the origin of a building is determined, the basic construction is studied: things such as brick, wood, nails, concrete, steel, pipes, wire, etc. To discover the origin of the universe, we look at the basic raw material — the most elementary parts — used for its construction. **(See fig. #11.)**

The atom is the basic elementary ingredient of the universe. It is composed of three basic units: space, matter and energy. **(See fig. #12.)**

Figure 10: Building blocks of creation

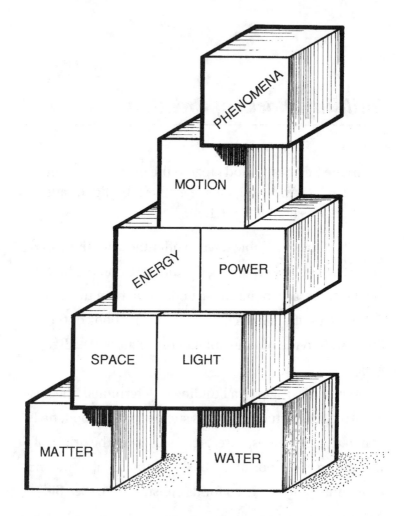

In the very first three verses of the first chapter of the first book of the Bible the building blocks of creation are listed.

Figure 11: Building materials for construction

To help determine the origin of a building, one would need to know the kinds of materials used in its construction: brick, wood, nails, concrete, steel, pipes, wire etc. To discover the origin of the universe, one also looks for the basic materials, the most elementary parts, used in its construction.

In Genesis One, God Reveals the Building Blocks of Creation

Heavens = Space

The Hebrew word *shamayim*, translated "heavens" in Genesis 1:1, can also be translated to mean "space" or "an expanse stretched out." So first, God created space.

Figure 12: The building blocks for the construction of an atom

Space, matter and energy are the three basic components of the atom.

Earth = Matter

The Hebrew Word *erets*, translated earth, can be translated to mean "matter" or "the substance from which things are formed." Secondly, God created matter.

In the beginning, God created all the matter in the universe. Genesis 1:2 indicates the material God had created was empty, formless and covered with darkness. The earth was yet without form. Like an unformed lump of clay, there was no shape — the raw material lay not yet fashioned. The earth was barren and lifeless; creation was not yet complete. The material, both of the Earth and things in space, was not yet consolidated into any sort of a working system.

The word "void" indicates pieces not organized nor assembled into any sort of purposeful pattern. Genesis 1:2 could be translated, "and the earthen matter was not arranged in any meaningful form." This signifies that the atoms had not yet been assembled, and the particles of the atom had not yet been activated into their swirling orbits. The atoms had been made, but were just lying there like the parts of a child's building set scattered across a table. **(See fig. #13.)** After creating matter *ex nihilo* (out of nothing), it then became necessary to organize matter into working systems.

Figure 13: God created in steps

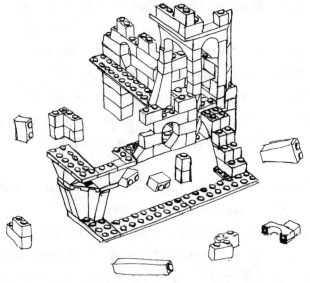

The word "void" in Genesis 1:2 indicates pieces not organized or assembled into any sort of purposeful pattern. The verse could be translated, "and the earthen matter was not arranged in any meaningful form." God first created two essential parts of the atom, space and matter; then He energized the atom by creating light.

Light = Energy

At the very instant God said, "Let there be light" (Gen. 1:3), the electrons began their atomic movement. The creation was energized as He spoke those words! Light is the most fundamental form of energy.[2]

We think of light as something we can see with our eyes, but actually what we can see is only a tiny part of light. Light encompasses much more than just visible light. It includes sound waves, radio waves, television waves, X rays, ultraviolet waves, gamma rays, etc., all of which make up what is called the electromagnetic spectrum. This spectrum is the breakdown of different wavelengths of energy. **(See fig. #14.)**

We live in a sea of waves. Not the usual type of water waves to which we are accustomed, but a sea of electromagnetic waves. Some of these waves go through us, others bounce off us, while others pass by us as if we never existed. Some are electric waves and some are magnetic waves. Whether of a high or a low frequency, these waves travel together at a speed of 186,000 miles per second in a vacuum.

Particles, called electrons, whirl around the nucleus billions of times every millionth of a second. They move at the speed of light. Such speed gives an indication of how quickly God spoke the universe into existence. It didn't require the billions of years evolutionism proposes. God

2   All the electromagneticforce systems (all types of energy except gravity and the nuclear forces) sre essentially different forms of light energy operating at different wave lengths. Even the nuclear forces involve the velocity of light

Figure 14: "Let there be light"

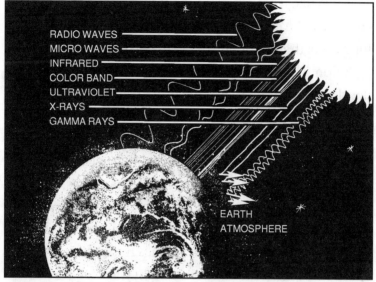

RADIO WAVES
MICRO WAVES
INFRARED
COLOR BAND
ULTRAVIOLET
X-RAYS
GAMMA RAYS

EARTH
ATMOSPHERE

At the very instant God said, "Let there be light" in Genesis 1:3, the entire electromagnetic spectrum was created, including not only visible light, but other forms of energy such as radio and microwaves, infrared rays, gamma rays, x rays and ultraviolet rays.

spoke it into formation in an instant.

As God's Spirit moved over the face of the waters (Gen. 1:2), the Hebrew word *rachaph* translated "moved" is used only three times in the Bible. In Deuteronomy 32:11, it is translated "fluttereth" and refers to a mother eagle beating her wings back and forth as she hovers over her young. We are told she does this in order to get her young airborne. In Jeremiah 23:9 it is translated "shake" and refers to trembling — the kind of trembling one does when nervous or chilled.

Thus, the movement of God's Spirit on the face of

the waters seems to have involved an intense motion
— much like what occurs in the fertilization of the human
cell. Once the egg is fertilized, it lays there motionless
for a time; then, suddenly it begins to undergo great
agitation. These pulsating movements result in the cell's
development. Similarly, in the process of creation when
God's Spirit moved on the face of the unformed earth and
waters, a new world was formed.

The word *rachaph* in the above Bible verses, implies
a rapid back and forth motion. Thus, it can be assumed
that when God's Spirit began to move, there was a similar
motion. In modern scientific terminology the translation
would be "vibrated." Science teaches transmission of
energy is in the form of waves — light waves — waves
in motion. Waves typically move rapidly back and forth.
The first impartation of energy to the universe could be
described as the vibrating movement of the Spirit of God
Himself. When God said, "Let there be light," the universe
was energized and motion was established by the "Prime
Mover."

The movement of God's Spirit also is mentioned in
the New Testament when "holy men of God spoke *as
they were* moved by the Holy Spirit" (II Pet 1:21 NKJV).
Here, the word "moved" is the Greek word *phero*, which
is the root word for the Greek word *epiphero* used in
the Septuagint (Greek translation of the Old Testament)
translated as "moved" in Genesis 1:2. [*Epiphero* means to
judicially superinduce or adduce; to bear upon.] Just as

God moved and energized the creation of the universe, so He later empowered His prophets of old, and through His Word He energizes men to become new creations, born again and full of His power and Spirit.

Within the first three verses of Scripture, God tells us about the foundational building blocks of His creation: space, matter and energy — known as the basic components of the atom. The Bible, even though it was written several thousand years ago, identifies the structure of an atom as we understand it today.

The historical context of the Genesis account of creation was of particular importance to the Jewish people during the Babylonian captivity, where they remained captives for many decades. They looked to God's Word for their source of truth. Today, we must also look to God's Word as the source of truth in a day where humanistic thought and atheistic evolutionism thrive. The absence of scientific error in the Word of God is astounding, especially when we study other ancient writings and sees so many obvious scientific blunders.

Visible light accounts for only a very small range of the entire spectrum. If you picture the entire light spectrum as notes on a piano, visible light would take up slightly less than an octave. The electromagnetic spectrum has such a huge range of frequencies that a piano would not have the normal eight octaves, but would have a mind-boggling 80 octaves. The keyboard would be 42 feet long with the "visible light" notes near octave number 52. This would truly be a *grand* piano, one that only God could design, construct and play.

Light, then, is energy — energy for atoms. So when God said, "Let there be light," energy was set in motion, and the particles of the atoms became swirling, miniature galaxies. Matter became a working system. **(See fig. #15.)**

Within the first three verses of Scripture, God tells us about the foundational building blocks of His creation: Space, matter and energy — all recently discovered as the basic components of the atom. The Bible, though written several thousand years ago, identifies the structure of an atom as we understand it today.

It is here that we see a parallel between the way in

Figure 15: The incredible atom

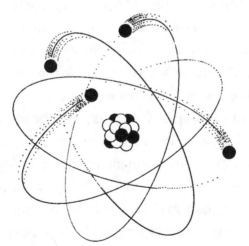

The atom is a swirling, miniature galaxy of energy. When God said, "Let there be light," energy was set in motion, and the particles of the atom became a working system.

which God spoke and created light and life in the physical realm by the words of His mouth, and the way Jesus, the Word and the Light, brought forth life in the spiritual realm. We know that in the beginning when God created the physical heaven and the physical Earth, there was darkness over it (Gen. 1:2). Then the Spirit of God began moving and God said, "Let there be light," (Gen. 1:3) and there was light — light that would sustain life.

As a result of the violence and corruption of the evilness of unregenerate man, the Earth was then covered with spiritual darkness (Gen. 6:11, 12). God saw that the darkness was not good. As the creation of light through the spoken word in Genesis dealt with the physical darkness, so God confronted spiritual darkness by sending Jesus as the Light — life-producing Light:

> In the beginning was the Word, and the Word was with God, and the Word was God. He was with God in the beginning. Through him all things were made; without him nothing was made that has been made. In him was life, and that life was the light of men. The light shines in darkness, but the darkness has not understood it (Jn. 1:1-5).

Christ is not only the Creator of the physical heavens and the physical Earth, He is the Light of the world and in Him there is life. After God created man, darkness came over his spirit as a result of his sin. By the release of His Word there was Light, resurrection and eternal life. It all happened because God spoke the Word and the Word was

Light and Life that overcame the darkness and barrenness of the world.

The Godhead Revealed

Interestingly, different aspects of the electromagnetic spectrum are revealed in the Godhead. For example, much of the electromagnetic spectrum is completely imperceptible to the five senses of man; this would represent Father God. The narrow belt of the light spectrum apparent to the eye is the visible color spectrum. This represents God revealing Himself in the flesh as the Messiah Whom we know as Christ Jesus. Finally, there is a part of the spectrum known as infrared light, which can't be seen by the eye, but can be felt by the body. This represents the Holy Spirit, Whom we cannot see, but Whose presence we can sense.

Advancing this concept, science now defines the universe in five terms: Time, space, matter, power and motion. (Science is slowly coming into line with the Bible.) Chapter one of the Book of Genesis revealed this truth to the Hebrews around 3,500 years ago, "In the beginning (time) God created the heavens (space) and the earth (matter). ... And the Spirit (power) of God was moving (motion) over the surface of the waters" (Gen. 1:1, 2 NAS).

The Bible is consistently clear in relating that God created the universe from nothing and did so without taxing His powers or energy. (See Psalm 33:6, 9 and

Hebrews 11:3.) The rest of Genesis chapter one also supports the ancient Christian doctrine that God was alone at the beginning and created the universe from nothing (*creation ex nihilo*). He did not require some preexistent substance. By creating light and darkness and by calling forth a land mass from the waters (see verses 9-10), God actually created time and space.

CHAPTER FIVE

The Most Incredible Substance in the Universe

... The Spirit of God was moving over the surface of the waters (Gen. 1:2 NAS).

In an immense universe stretching through the vastness of space, our nearest neighbor is the moon. Man has walked on its dry, dusty surface and we know with certainty it is barren, desolate — devoid of even the "simplest" form of life. What a tremendous contrast this is to our present home, the Earth — a planet of striking beauty, teeming with life.

What makes the difference? Why is the moon barren and desolate while the Earth abounds with life? Water makes the difference! **(See fig. #16.)** There's nothing else quite like it in the universe. Earth's surface is blessed with a special concentration of liquid water, unknown to other planets. Water — this odorless, colorless and tasteless substance — is one of the most unique chemicals in the world. Even *Science Digest,* an evolutionary magazine, recognizes the uniqueness of water and makes mention of

Figure 16: The desolate moon

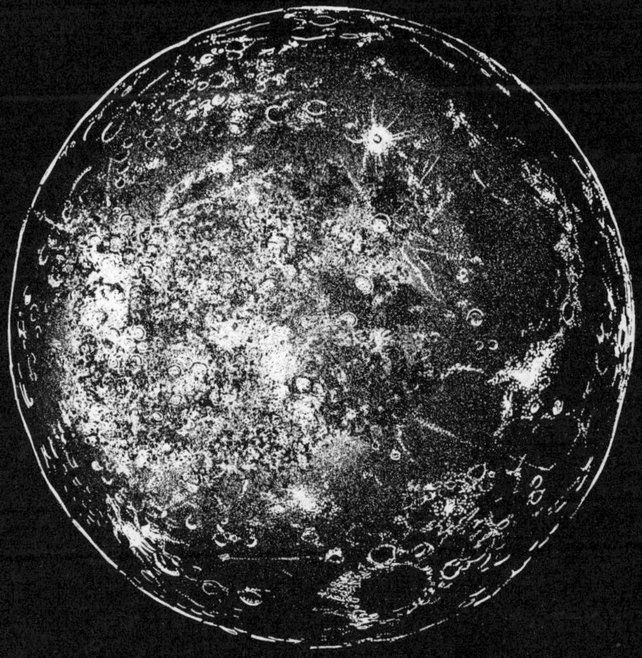

The barrenness and desolation of the moon testifies to the significance of water. Where there is water, there is life; where there is no water, there is no life.

it in its May 1982 issue:

> Though we cook with it, clean with it — and largely consist of it — few of us truly understand the nature of water. This odd compound is one of the most complex on earth. ... It is the most pervasive — and most essential — compound on Earth. ... This talented substance helps to balance the planet's climate, run its machines and support its life forms. That it may also baffle those who try to

unravel its secrets is merely another example of its remarkable complexity.

When water molecules are looked at on the microscopic level, they exhibit something called the hydrophobic effect, which gives water the unique ability to shape proteins and nucleic acids in DNA. From a molecular standpoint, "The various properties of water are nothing short of miraculous," writes Michael Corey in *God and the New Cosmology.* "No other compound even comes close to duplicating its many life-supporting properties."[9]

Scientists know the necessity of water for life. When a space probe lands on another planet, one of the things it looks for is water or moisture to see if it is possible for life forms to exist.

Earth is the only planet in the solar system with huge bodies of water; 70 percent of its surface area consists of oceans, seas and lakes. **(See fig. #17.)** Water in liquid form cannot exist on Mars, for instance, because there is not enough atmospheric pressure to allow it to remain a liquid. Mars, then, is a cold, desert-like planet with no possibility for life, as we know it, to exist. The few planets having water contain only moisture floating as vapor on their surface, not large bodies of liquid water as on Earth. Recently, scientists discovered there is water out in the emptiness of interstellar space.[10] This is quite interesting in light of Scripture. The Bible has been giving us clues

Figure 17: Water — There is nothing like it

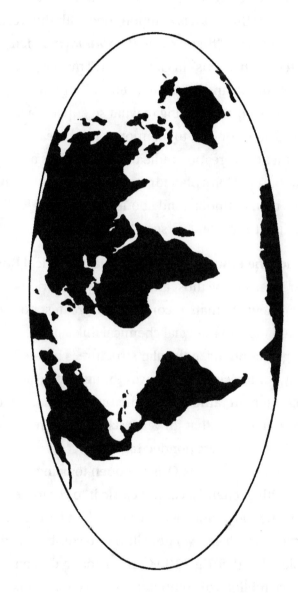

The earth is the only planet in the solar system with huge bodies of water; 70% of its surface area consists of water. Water has tremendous significance and value, not only in the physical realm, but in the spiritual: "But whoever drinks the water I give him will never thirst. Indeed, the water I give him will become in him a spring of water welling up to eternal life." (John 4:14 NIV)

all along. The Hebrew word for waters is *mayim*. The first instance of this word is compounded with the word *sham*, which means "there" or "in it." *Shamayim*, then is translated as "heavens" in Genesis 1:1. This passage reveals that the expanse of the heavens inherently includes water, corresponding to what scientists have recently learned. For God to mention water here in the initial moments of creation indicates that it plays a very important part in God's plan for creation. What is it that God wants man to understand about water when He mentions it in the second verse of the Bible?

Water Holds the Power to Form a Special Chemical Bond

Water is one of the most amazing and mysterious molecules known to man. It contains the greatest power of any liquid to form a special chemical link called the hydrogen bond. Its molecular structure is bonded so strongly, until recent times it was thought to be an indivisible element rather than a chemical compound. Its structure is so unique that for years scientists were baffled as to how its atoms were bonded together.

The water molecule, H_2O, is not open to being tampered with. A chemist cannot cause it to combine with other chemicals and elements in order to form new elements. Its properties will not allow it to combine with other molecules. **(See fig. #18.)** Carbon and hydrogen can produce millions of combinations — so many that even computers have been unable to figure out exactly

Figure 18:   The water molecule will not combine with other molecules

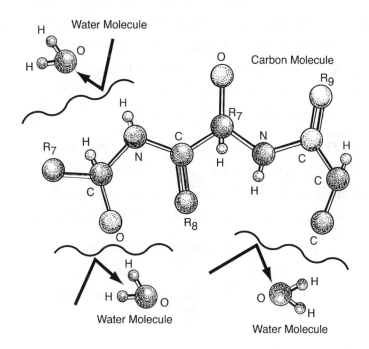

Uniquely, the water molecule will not combine with other elements to form new elements. Chemists can make millions of new combinations with other elements, but not with the water molecule. God had a special purpose in mind when He created water: life.

how many combinations there can be. However, when it comes to hydrogen and oxygen, the elements that make up the water molecule, there are only two ways in which these elements can be combined: H_2O (water) and H_2O_2 (hydrogen peroxide, an antiseptic). It appears that right from the beginning God had a purpose in mind when He created the water molecule, and that was for life.

The peculiar properties of water seem to have been designed expressly for the purpose of making the Earth hospitable to the existence of life. The water molecule is "V-shaped" rather then symmetrical. This strange arrangement of the atoms in the water molecule allows water to have unusual characteristics — all for the purpose of sustaining life. **(See fig. #19.)**

Water Has the Ability to Expand When It Freezes

Even though water may seem common to us, its properties are distinctive; it is totally out of step with the laws that govern other chemicals. For example, most

Figure 19: The bond angle of a water molecule

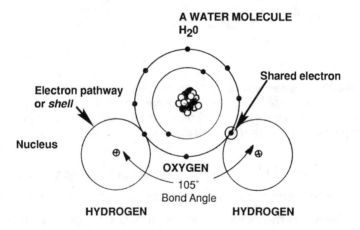

The water molecule has some very unusual characteristics which are out of step with the characteristics of other elements. If it were not for the atypical attributes of the water molecule, life would not be possible. The Creator, in his wisdom, designed the water molecule with the purpose of sustaining life.

elements — liquids, solids or gases — will contract when cooled and expand when heated. However, once water reaches 36° F., it reacts in just the reverse manner, which is very important to life. Once it reaches 36° F., water begins to expand until it freezes. Its molecules arrange themselves in a manner causing the mass to swell.

If water contracted as it cooled, ice would become heavier than liquid water and would sink. All life would perish in lakes and rivers because the water would become one solid mass of ice during the freezing winter months. Even the oceans would be affected; the ocean bottoms would be extremely cold and many fish would die. Eventually, much of the oceans would continue to freeze until completely solid, killing all marine life.

But because of the unusual quirk within the water molecule, which causes it to expand when it freezes, it occupies more space than liquid water without weighing more and thus it floats. As the ice covers the surface of water, it acts as a layer of insulation or a blanket, protecting the water and the life below from freezing.

Water's Liquid Temperature Range Allows for Life

Water has a liquid temperature range at which enzymes (complex organic substances that cause chemical reactions in the living cell) and other life molecules can exist. It boils and freezes at a point totally out of line with the boiling and freezing points of other elements, which is very important to the survival of life;

Figure 20: Boiling and freezing characteristics of water

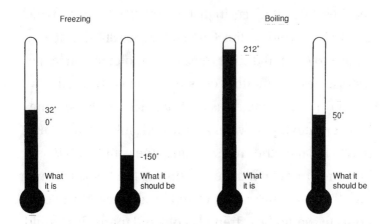

Water boils and freezes at points totally out of line with the boiling and freezing points of other elements. If water followed the same rules other elements do, life would be difficult, if not impossible.

otherwise, under the conditions of temperature and pressure of our Earth, we wouldn't have water in liquid form. If water followed the normal rules, it would boil at about 50° F. and freeze at about –150° F. But instead, it boils at 212° F. and freezes a 32° F. **(See fig. #20.)**

Water Has the Highest Capacity for Heat Absorption of Any Liquid

As beautiful as the ocean can be, especially at sunset, it seems to be a wasted expanse that could be used for additional living space and agricultural development. If the oceans were greatly reduced in size, perhaps there wouldn't be destructive tsunamis (huge waves caused by earthquakes) and hurricanes. However, it is now known that if 75 percent of the world were not covered with water, the atmospheric water cycle would not work properly. Our climate would not support plant and animal life because it would be dry and unpredictable.

Since water is an excellent temperature stabilizer, the large oceans on the Earth are vital to our survival. Water can absorb large amounts of heat without much alteration occurring in its own temperature. Its heat-absorption speed is extremely rapid — about 10 times as fast as that of steel.

During the day, when the sun's rays are pouring down on the Earth, the seas rapidly soak up a great deal of the heat, keeping Earth fairly cool. At night, oceans release the vast amounts of heat they have soaked up during the day, which, combined with atmospheric effects, keeps the surface of Earth from getting too cold at night. Therefore, if it were not for the tremendous amount of water on Earth, there would be far greater day and night temperature variations. Many parts of the Earth's surface would be hot enough to boil water in the day (like the 275° F. temperature that often bakes our moon) and then cold enough to freeze water at night. **(See fig. #21.)**

Water Has the Greatest Capacity as a Solvent of Any Liquid

Water comes closer than any other liquid to being a universal solvent. Given enough time, it will dissolve almost any other substance. Most other liquids will react and combine to form a new component. Were it not for

Figure 21: Water — An excellent temperature stabilizer

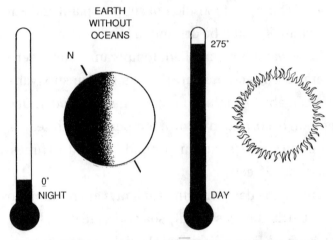

the ability of water to dissolve the chemicals and minerals

Since water is an excellent temperature stabilizer, the large oceans on the earth are vital to the survival of life. Without the large oceans, many parts of the earth's surface would be hot enough to boil water in the day and cold enough to freeze it at night.

with which it comes in contact, man, animals and plants would not get the nutrients they need. In digestion, water is what helps to dissolve minerals and carry them to all parts of the body. In fact, water is absolutely essential — in liquid form — for all the key systems of life. The digestive, reproductive, circulatory and respiratory systems of our bodies are all dependent on water. It is the only possible solvent (having the power to dissolve) for living cells.

Water is Essential for Life

In a very personal way, water means everything to man. The average human body is 70 percent water, and since man is constantly losing it, if he does not replace it, he will die. **(See fig. # 22.)** The water in our blood carries it through the 100,000 miles of arteries, capillaries and veins in our bodies. Water plays a major role in the digestion of food, lubricates our joints and regulates body heat. It is

Figure 22: Water and man

The average healthy body consists of 70% water. Without replenishing this vital element, man would die in just a few days.

not only humans who are composed mostly of water; a major portion of every living thing on the Earth is made of water.

Spiritual Water Is Essential for Spiritual Life

In Genesis 1:2, the Spirit of God is mentioned in relation to water. It cannot be a coincidence that here, in the second verse of the Bible, we find water and God's Spirit mentioned together. Just as water is essential for physical life, so the Spirit is essential for spiritual life. The fact that God's Spirit interacted with water at the beginning of creation, amplifies the life-giving qualities of each. Water is symbolic of God's Word. We are refreshed by it. It is also symbolic of salvation for without either water or salvation we are dead.

The apostle John seems to have a special interest in water as seen in the following stories: John baptizing in the Jordan (Jn. 1:31-33); the ceremonial water pots used in Cana of Galilee (Jn. 2:6); Jacob's well (Jn. 4); the pools of Bethesda (Jn. 5); and the pools of Siloam (Jn. 9).[3]

In Jerusalem, John portrays Jesus as the living water of salvation, which He alone can give. Jesus' encounter with Nicodemus likewise reveals the significance of water. "No one can enter the Kingdom of God unless he is born of water and the Spirit" (Jn. 3:5). Jesus was stating that there is no entrance into God's Kingdom without being born or being baptized in the water of the Spirit. Jesus offers salvation in the gift of the Holy Spirit, as it is the Spirit

Himself who is the living water. Jesus was announcing Himself as the source of "the rivers of living water."

The properties in water were not acquired through a process of random chance, but were designed right from the beginning by the Master Designer, God. Having created water with such tremendous significance on life, He parallels the necessity of water for physical life and living water for eternal life: Jesus is the living water. Where water runs, there is life, and where it does not run, there is death.

John tells us how to be born of the Spirit in Christ's encounter with the Samaritan woman; it is a vivid expression of this life-giving water:

> Jesus answered and said to her, "If you knew the gift of God, and who it is who says to you, 'Give Me a drink,' you would have asked Him, and He would have given you living water" (John 4:10 NAS).

Jesus' analogy is the living water from the artesian well of the Spirit springing up to provide eternal life. In Isaiah 12:3, we read, "With joy you will draw water from the wells of salvation." John tells how Jesus at the Feast of Tabernacles cries out, "If anyone is thirsty, let him come to me and drink" (Jn. 7:37, 38).

Right from the beginning of God's Word we are told of the unusual part water played in His creative work during the creation. On the very first day of creation, we see God incorporating the building blocks for life into our world:

Space, matter, energy and then, the unique, life-giving substance — water (Gen. 1: 1-3). The parallel between the significance of physical water (without which our body cannot live) and the living water offered to man by God (without which our spirit cannot live) emphasizes that we cannot receive eternal life without receiving the living water of God. Thus, in Genesis 1:2, we are given the first glimpse of the significance God gives to water. Water, which is essential for physical life, is likewise essential for life with the Spirit; it is this life that provides eternal life.

Calling Things into Existence

In Genesis chapter one, we find that creation was accomplished in a series of steps. In verse two, we find that Earth was in a state of incompleteness. God was still working to complete His plan of creation. So God said (in essence), "Let the earth (matter) receive light (energy) so that it can bring forth its finished product and purpose — life and mankind."

In verse two, we read that God's Spirit moved upon the face of the waters. The Hebrew word for "move" is *Rachaph*. *Rachaph* means "moving" or "to brood over" as a mother hen broods over her eggs. The root meaning is to breed, to give birth to, reproduction and fertilization. God was calling forth life in the physical realm by "hovering and brooding over."

In Psalm 90:2 we read:

Before the mountains were born or you brought

the spirit by intercession and travail when there is a need to bring life from barrenness and lifelessness. The creative energy of God can then be released to manifest new life. This is the birthing process. Push in travail as God did with the original creation. Likewise, disciples of Christ the Creator are to go and bring forth new creations.

CHAPTER SIX

The Mind-Boggling Atom

By faith we understand that the universe was formed at God's command, so that what is seen was not made out of what was visible (Heb. 11:3).

Fortuitous "Coincidences"

Take another example: The structure of an atom. Everything in the universe is made of atoms, from the stars in the farthest heavens to the cells in the human body — even the atom itself is a bundle of fortuitous "coincidences." Within the atom, the neutron is just slightly more massive than the proton, which means that

Figure 23: *Parts of the atom and their relative sizes*

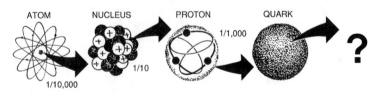

The Bible, in addition to revealing space, matter and energy as the building blocks of creation, makes some remarkable statements about the atom.

free neutrons (those not trapped within an atom) can decay and turn into protons. If things were reversed — if it were the proton that was larger and had a tendency to decay — the very structure of the universe would be impossible. And why is the neutron larger than the proton? No one knows. There is no physical cause to explain why the neutron is larger. It is simply a fact. Apparently, the only "reason" for the difference in size is that it allows the universe to exist and to support life.[xi]

The Atom: An Electrical Phenomenon

The atom plays a vital part in God's creation. **(See fig. #23.)** All matter is comprised of atoms. The atom is

Figure 24: The laws of electricity

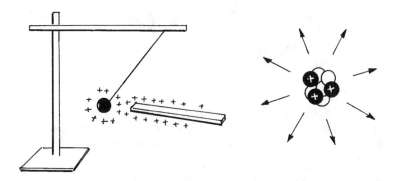

One of the laws of electricity is that like charges repel one another. Since the prorons inside the nucleus of an atom are all positively charged, they should repel one another and scatter. But because of a mysterious binding force holding them together, they do not. This binding force is so powerful, the discovery of its properties has given scientests the key to atomic power.

Figure 25: Splitting the atom

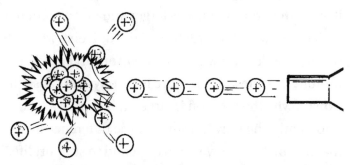

600,000 ELECTRON-VOLT PRORONS (6,660 MILES PER SECOND) WILL NOT PENETRATE THE PROTECTIVE SHIELD

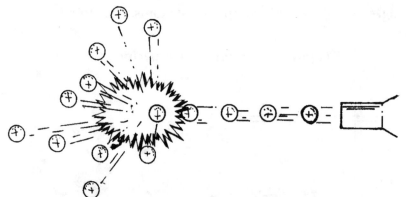

IT REQUIRES 900,000 ELECTRON-VOLT PROTONS (8,170 MILES PER SECOND) TO PENETRATE THE PROTECTIVE SHIELD IN ORDER TO SMASH THE NUCLEUS AND TO RELEASE ITS CONTENTS.

In costly technical machinery known as supercolliders, tiny particles are accelerated at velocity near the speed of light in order to break through the binding force which holds the atom together to probe its secrets.

made up of electrons and protons, which are not really solids, but positive and negative charges of electricity. The atom has a dense center called the nucleus. Inside the nucleus are the neutrons and protons. The neutrons have no electrical charge and are therefore neutral; but the protons have positive charges.

One of the laws of electricity is that like charges repel one another. Therefore, since the protons inside the nucleus are all positive charges, they should repel one another and scatter, but for some reason they do not. (See fig. #24.) There is a binding force, not yet understood, holding them together. In addition, when the neutrons of the atom are smashed, they scatter into parts that become electrons and protons and a multitude of other kinds of particles — the number of which staggers the imagination. (See fig. #25.)

The Atom Contains Unthinkable Power

In just one railroad ticket there are enough atoms to supply sufficient energy to power a diesel train around the world several times. (See fig. #26.) The atomic energy available in the average school textbook is equivalent to the energy output of Hoover Dam for one year — or enough energy to power the electrical needs of an average home for a million years. In one human breath there is enough atomic energy to fly a spacecraft to the moon. The atomic energy in one pound of any kind of matter, such as water, is the equivalent of the burning of 1½ million tons

Figure 26: The power of an atom

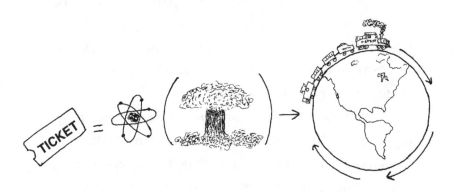

The power within an atom is almost beyond man's comprehension. For instance, the potential power within the atoms contained in just one railroad ticket is enough energy to power a diesel train around the world several times.

of coal. **(See fig. #27.)** All of this energy is stored in the tiny particles of which matter is composed.

Electrons Move With Unbelievable Speed

The particles called electrons (which have negative electrical charges) whirl around the nucleus of the atom billions of times every millionth of a second. **(See fig. #28.)** These opposite charges of electricity attract each other; the protons and electrons pull at each other, keeping the electrons from dispersing. Where did this electrical charge come from that holds the atoms together in such a specific manner? What force causes these electrons to orbit the nucleus of the atom at such an unbelievable speed?

Figure 27: The potential power in a liter of water

The potential atomic energy in one liter of water is equivalent to the power that one and a half million tons of coal could provide.

Figure 28: The speed of the electron

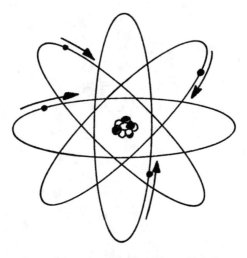

Around the nucleus of the atom tiny particles called electrons whirl billions of times every millionth of a second.

The Mysterious Binding Force

What is the binding force of an atom? Scientists have discovered this binding force and its properties can be worked out mathematically, but they do not know what it is or how it got there. Recently, they have found two new forces within the atom called the pi-mesons. They believe the pi-mesons may be the energy holding things together. It is totally invisible; it can't be seen, felt, tasted or weighed. But it is there! What is this nuclear glue?

Man can continue to observe and research the atom, discovering more about how it works and of what it is comprised. Yet the question still remains: Who is the creator and the controller of these incredible forces? Did it all come about by unintelligent chance or was intelligence involved? If so, whose?

> ... In him (Christ) *all things hold together* (Col. 1:17, emphasis added).

> The Son is the radiance of God's glory and the exact representation of his being, *sustaining all things* by his powerful word (Heb. 1:3, emphasis added).

Walking Through Walls

A model of the hydrogen atom could be made by taking a bowling ball to represent the nucleus. Then place a pea, representing the electron, 10 miles away from the nucleus. **(See fig. #29.)** The amount of space between is startling. The distance between these swirling particles called electrons and the nucleus is about the same ratio of distance between the Earth and the sun.

In other words, the atom is mostly composed of space, and matter is composed of atoms. Thus, man is

Figure 29: The startling amount of space
in an atom

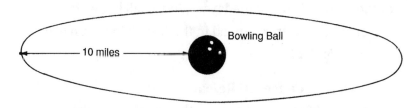

Atoms are composed of mostly space, which means that all matter
(including steel, which is very dense) is composed mostly of space.

mostly composed of space — or nonphysical substance. If the actual matter in a human body could be compressed into a ball, it would be smaller than the head of a pin. Considering the vast amount of space within each atom in proportion to the exceedingly small size of the protons and electrons, atoms should be able to pass through each other. Even steel is mostly space. All matter is primarily constructed of space so that the actual matter is really composed of literally invisible particles. Consider the following verse.

> ... We know that the world and the stars — in fact, all things — were made at God's command; and that they were all made from things that can't be seen (Heb. 11:3 LB).

Since atoms are composed mostly of space, why can't they pass through one another? It isn't the actual atoms that keep a person from walking through a wall, but the invisible forces surrounding the atom. These powerful forces prohibit passage of other atoms.

Jesus was able to walk through walls after His resurrection. He has power to overrule the binding force of the atom. Maybe someday we, too, shall know the secret, when we are changed in the "twinkling of an eye ... " (I Cor. 15:51, 52).

Planned (But Canceled) Research

Jeremiah declared long ago that man will never completely search out and understand the foundations of

the Earth (matter) and the measurements of the heavens
(Jer. 31:37).

Man will continue to probe and search, and will
make some discoveries. The planned construction of the
"supercollider" in Texas was estimated to cost $6 billion
and was to be 54 miles in circumference. This circular
instrument was to give colliding protons the energy of 40
trillion electron volts. The power was to be so great that
it would hopefully have been able to break through the
invisible force surrounding the atom and open up (split)
the atom. Scientists wanted to investigate the structure
of the atom, as well as particles inside the atom not yet
understood.

Man has unraveled the atom by probing into its
nucleus, discovering the protons and the neutrons. But
what infinitesimal element yet lies undiscovered inside
the protons and the neutrons? Since the project was
canceled, we will never know if this atom-smasher, the
"supercollider," would have been able to reveal more
about the fundamental components of matter.

The Final Atomic Explosion

It appears that the evolutionists' theory of a "Big
Bang" may have some validity after all; however, they
simply missed the timing of its occurrence. Instead of
taking place at the beginning of creation, it may take
place at the end of time.

… All these things shall be dissolved … (II Pet. 3:11

KJV).

The Word of God states that at the end of the world all things will be dissolved or "unloosed." Scientific research regarding the atom reveals that all God would have to do is remove the binding force from the atoms, and the whole Earth would blow up like a giant atom bomb. **(See fig. #30.)** The "supercollider" experiments were able to create tiny fireballs 400 million times as hot as the sun as a result of smashing electrons into one another at almost the speed of light.

The realm of physics serves to demonstrate how God could destroy the world in an instant if He chose to do so.

Figure 30: The end of time

God's Word reveals that at the end of time, this creation will experience a nuclear holocaust in which "…all things shall be dissolved…" (II Pet. 3:11). Scientific research reveals that all that God would have to do is remove the binding force holding atoms together, and the entire universe would blow up in a brief moment

God created the universe in a brief moment; and in a brief moment, He can destroy it.

The Atom: A Force Unequaled

Tucked away in the most elementary, infinitesimal part of creation, there is a force unequaled by any other. All that is necessary for God to "pull the plug" would be for Him to remove the binding force holding the atom together. This creation could instantly vanish in an atomic blast.

New Heavens and a New Earth

The Bible speaks of a future, supernatural intervention of the Creator in His creation in which He will destroy the present creation and form a new one — new heavens and a new Earth where only righteousness dwells and which shall continue without end.

> And I saw a new heaven and a new earth; for the first heaven and the first earth passed away, and there is no longer *any* sea (Rev. 21:1 NAS).

> For behold I create new heavens and a new earth; and the former things shall not be remembered or come to mind (Isa.65:17 NAS).

> But according to His promise we are looking for new heavens and a new earth, in which righteousness dwells (II Pet. 3:13 NAS).

The Donkey Award

The words of I Corinthians 1:20, "Where is the wise man? Where is the scholar? Where is the philosopher of this age? Has not God made foolish the wisdom of this world?" could not be more accurate in the light of the evolutionary delusion regarding the end.

One evolutionary theory proposes that the end will be as follows: The universe will continue to expand indefinitely, and the stars, in time, will consume the vast supply of hydrogen. Star formation will slow and then stop, and the last stars will blink out, bringing an end to all activity in the universe.

Some evolutionists have a more optimistic belief. They believe there is enough matter in the universe to halt the expansion; and that the onrushing, star-filled galaxies will eventually slow to a stop, then begin speeding back through space until they crash together to re-form the primordial atom. Then the giant atom will explode again, sending its fragments flying outward to re-create the cosmos and life itself in an oscillating, never-ending cycle. Sounds like a spin-off of Hinduism and reincarnation.

One evolutionist, Greenstein, hasn't made up his mind as to which theory he believes is correct. However, his statement substantiates the truth of I Corinthians 1:20, "… Has not God made foolish the wisdom of the world?" Greenstein said, "I find a certain pleasure and honor in belonging to the universe of stars, of these events that have created the materials of which the Earth and I are made."

Some suggest it is better to have been living for a season, even for a moment, than not to have lived at all. No wonder there is such despair and hopelessness in the world today, with "educated" men making such absurd statements.

> The fool says in his heart, "There is no God" (Psa. 53: 1).

CHAPTER SEVEN

A 20ᵗʰ Century Adult Fairy Tale: Spontaneous Generation

Molecules to Man

> You alone are the LORD. You made the heavens, even the highest heavens, and all their starry host, the earth and all that is on it, the seas and all that is in them. You give life to everything, and the multitudes of heaven worship you (Neh. 9:6).

When it comes to the origin of life, there are only two alternatives: Special creation by a supernatural cause or spontaneous generation, which suggests "life" simply arose without any intelligent cause behind it. **(See fig. #31.)** There is no third alternative! Some are proposing life came from outer space, but even if that were a possibility, the question still remains: "How did life come about? By unintelligent blind chance or divine supernatural intervention?"

Up to now the focus has been on the span of time before life came on the scene. We compared creation accounts in chapter one. In chapter two, we saw the

Figure 31: Evolution's concept of the origin of life

According to evolutionism, unintelligent forces such as lightning, volcanic eruptions, and a batch of chemicals resulted in the appearance of life on earth. This is known as the Theory of Spontaneous Generation.

importance of the battle over origins between creationists and evolutionists. In chapter three, we took a look at the beginning of creation from a biblical perspective and compared it to the evolutionary "Cosmic Egg" theory. In chapter four, we investigated the building blocks of creation and how each harmonizes with Scripture. In chapter five, we studied the unique structure of the water molecule for sustaining life and saw its corresponding spiritual significance to eternal life. Finally, in chapter six, we delved deeper into the incredible design and power of the atom, which gave us insight into the force that holds the universe together and its future end.

Having looked at the beginning of creation, we now consider the beginning of life according to the Bible in contrast to the theory of evolutionism. Evolutionists suggest that an unattended batch of chemicals came to life spontaneously and mutated into thousands of freaks of various sizes, shapes and colors that have since overrun planet Earth. **(See fig. #32.)** This is one of the wildest fairy tales of the 20th century. It is nothing more than pagan mythology that Satan has devised to satisfy the heart and soul of a rebellious creature who stands before the Creator of the universe and shakes his fist saying, "I don't want you to tell me how to run my life." God, with tears in His eyes and love in His heart, says, "Okay." God will never force His love on an individual. However, He will separate such individuals from those who wish to follow His plan of redemption. This separation will take place at the last

Figure 32: "From goo to you, by way of the zoo"

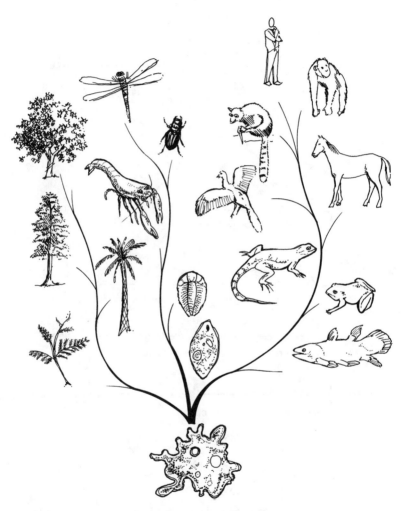

The absurd theory of spontaneous generation suggests that after life appeared on earth, it began to mutate into thousands of freaks of various sizes, shapes and colors which we now know as birds, fish, mammals and insects.

Figure 33: *The mythological stages of spontaneous generatoin*

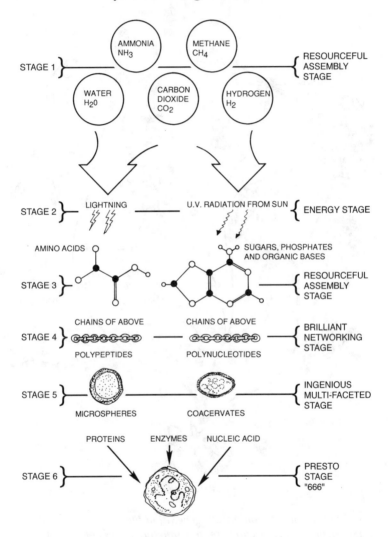

Evolutionists believe a "soup" of various chemicals went through a series of complicated transformations and eventually a living cell appeared.

judgment (Rev. 20: 11-15).

Evolutionists Propose Spontaneous Generation

How did life come about? Evolutionists propose
a theory called spontaneous generation: a "soup"
comprised of various chemicals somehow produced life.
Supposedly, on the early Earth the oceans and chemicals
got together and formed the first living cell. **(See fig.
#33.)** Now that was no small accomplishment, because
the simplest single-cell organism we know anything
about has, in its genes and chromosomes, about as much
information as there are letters in the world's largest
library — a trillion letters — and this all supposedly was
directed by blind, unintelligent chance. And as a matter of
fact, the single-celled radiolarian has 1,600 chromosomes!
That's a great deal of genetic material for a protozoan
— which means "first life." **(See fig. #34.)**

Although the simplest of all organisms is very
complex, the protozoan is comprised of scores of
functioning parts, each performing a specific function
and all working together for the good of the whole.
Remove any one of these functioning parts, and the whole
organism dies. By observing the order of the organism,
the purpose of each part, and the interdependence of
the parts, one would never conclude that it happened by
chance.

Evolutionary scientists have combined all their
intelligence and, through the use of chemicals one

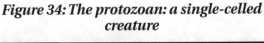

Figure 34: The protozoan: a single-celled creature

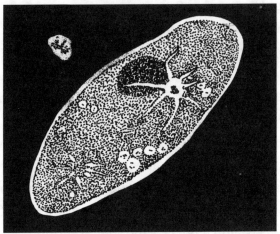

The simplest of all organisms, the protozoan, is comprised of scores of sophisticated functioning parts, each performing a specific function and all working together for the good of the whole.

million times more concentrated that those found in natural form on the Earth, have tried to prove life arose spontaneously — without any intelligent involvement. They have come up empty-handed. Though their theory has been popularized for a number of years, it has never been observed anywhere on Earth; there is not one shred of evidence in favor of it.

Evolutionists hold to the statement, "The present is the key to the past." However, if the present is the key to the past and yet spontaneous generation has never been observed in the present, why is it believed to have happened in the past?

Pasteur's Experiments Invalidate the Spontaneous Generation Theory

In the past, some people accepted the possibility life could generate spontaneously. They thought they saw evidence of such. For instance, when meat is left open and uncovered, maggots seem to appear out of nowhere. Pond water, it was believed, produced frogs.

Louis Pasteur, a famous chemist and bacteriologist of the 1800s, experimented with sterilization; he proved that once all organisms and microorganisms are dead, no such "spontaneous life" would occur. Once something is sterilized, life is impossible.

When the microscope was invented, it revealed the presence of all kinds of organisms invisible to the naked eye. The maggots were not appearing spontaneously; their eggs were just too small for the naked eye to see.

The Frog Prince

Suppose someone walks into your science laboratory at school wearing a purple robe with stars on it and a funny pointed hat, with a wand in his hand and claims that it is possible for a frog to become a prince in just a few seconds of time. He would be laughed at and ridiculed out of the classroom. However, if someone with a Ph.D., fuzzy gray hair and wire-rim glasses, came into your classroom wearing a white laboratory jacket and waving a pointer at a chalkboard, claiming that a frog became a prince of a man over millions of years of time, he might end up winning the Nobel Prize for science. In other words, by simply expanding the amount of time involved, a ridiculous notion has been accepted as a credible idea. **(See fig. # 35 a, b.)**

But that's not all of this amazing fantasy. The myth also claims that damages due to some outside influence — like cosmic rays — caused the first single cell to make a mistake in its reproduction mechanism. Gradually, one organism changed into another organism — all the way from a single cell to invertebrates like clams or starfish, and then to invertebrate fishes, amphibians, reptiles, birds, mammals and finally man: The product of billions of mistakes. This makes even less sense than some of the early, pagan accounts of creation, which were discussed in chapter one.

Can Life Be Produced in the Lab?

Has life been produced in a test-tube from non-living material? Absolutely not! In May of 1953, Dr. Stanley Miller and Dr. Sidney Fox published a paper in which they described the successful synthesis (formation) of an amino acid (a building block of the living cell). The news media sensationalized this experiment by announcing scientists had created "life." **(See fig. #36.)**

What Are Amino Acids?

Cells are the basic unit of all life. Each cell's structures are built mostly of proteins. A protein is a complicated chemical substance made up of smaller building blocks

Figure 35a: The tale of a toad: Part 1

Figure 35b: The tale of a toad: Part 1I

Figure 36:   The apparatus used by Drs. Miller and Fox in producing amino acids in the laboratory

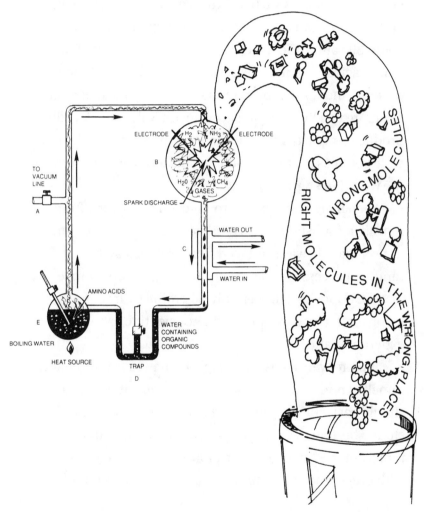

In 1953, amino acids (a building block of the living cell) were produced in a laboratory

called amino acids; there are about 20 different common amino acids. Each amino acid consists of various chemical elements such as hydrogen, oxygen, nitrogen and carbon atoms. A medium-sized protein might include about 300 amino acids. The specific arrangement of these amino acids in sequences dictates the function of each protein. And it is the protein that makes up most of a cell's structure in a living organism. Though Miller and Fox did produce simple amino acids in their experiments, they were about as far from producing life as the east is from the west. **(See fig. #37.)**

Even if life is someday produced in a test-tube from non-living substances, this will not prove the evolutionary notion that life was produced from lifelessness, by random processes and chance. Actually, it would prove just the opposite: Life can only be produced from non-living matter by closely controlled, scientific, laboratory experimentation.

If there were a basic principle of matter that somehow impelled non-living substances toward life, its existence should easily be demonstrable in the laboratory. One should be able to create a chemical conglomeration to represent the "prehistoric primordial soup," then zap it with every kind of radiation known to man, and bingo: life.

During such an experiment, how many of the 2,000 enzymes (complex organic substances) necessary to produce life — which is still a zillion miles from becoming

Figure 37: *The cell and amino acid*

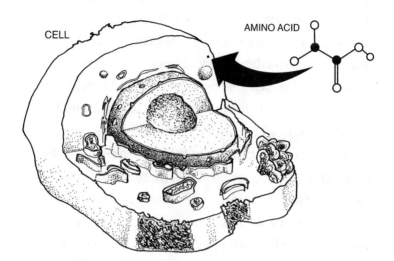

Investigation of the components that make up the cell reveal a degree of complexity unequaled by any structure in the universe. Amino acids have been synthesized in a laboratory; however, they are immeasurably simple in comparison to the cell itself. Comparing the cell to New York City, the amino acid would be like a single brick.

life — would be produced in a year's time? The answer is *none.* How can we be so sure? The answer is very simple. If it were possible, the experiment would long since have been accomplished by some exuberant evolutionist, and would be well-known throughout the world. The cost of such an experiment would be trivial compared to the cost of landing a man on the moon, though the significance would be equivalent. In short, there is not a shred of objective evidence to support the notion that life began in an organic "soup" here on the Earth.

Evolutionists Have the Public Duped

Somehow, evolutionists have duped the public into believing evolutionism is science. However, the evolutionary theory is a religious belief, not science. According to the dictionary, *science* is defined as "knowledge" which can be "observed and repeatedly tested." Evolutionism is not science, for it cannot be investigated in a laboratory. There were no human witnesses to the inception of life, no samples of original atmosphere or oceans. In short, there is no way of proving the idea of spontaneous generation.

We have also been led to believe one can set up apparatus in a laboratory to simulate the original atmosphere and oceans (the presumed, original conditions on the primeval Earth) to show how life may have formed millions of years ago. However, in doing this kind of experiment one could never prove life evolved by chance because intelligence is inserted into these experiments. Even if scientists were to actually create some form of life in the laboratory, this would have nothing to do with chance, but everything to do with intelligence. If it takes intelligence to attempt to form life the second time in the laboratory, then, obviously, it took intelligence for life to be created the first time. The more evolutionists use laboratory experimentation to try to prove life arose by chance, the more they are proving life arose by intelligent design.

The Evolutionists' Dilemma

With the evidence pointing to a fixed beginning for the universe, the evolutionists are really in a dilemma. They have poked fun at the Christians for believing God could create something out of nothing. Yet the only alternative to the creationist theory is eternal matter. Evolutionists claim that the Christians' belief in an eternal God Who creates miraculously is only a ridiculous assumption. However, the evolutionists believe a much more incredible (ridiculous) story. They believe that eternal matter somehow "miraculously" created life. **(See fig. # 38.)** As creationist Duane Gish noted, "It is unbelievable what the unbeliever has to believe to remain an unbeliever."

The Evolutionists' "Faith"

Believe it or not, the following are words of two distinguished and well-educated men:

> It became an accepted doctrine that life never rises except from life. So far as the actual evidence goes, this is still the only possible conclusion. But since it is a conclusion that seems to lead back to some supernatural creative act, it is a conclusion that scientific men find very difficult to accept.[xii]

> … The theory of evolution itself, a theory universally accepted, not because it can be proven by logically coherent evidence to be true, but because the only alternative, special creation, is clearly incredible.[xiii]

Figure 38: No "intelligence" at work

"Students, since I have just received my new supercomputer, I now believe I will be able to demonstrate how life could have evolved by chance without any intelligence sponsoring it. Watch carefully!"

How is it possible that such statements can be uttered by sophisticated scholars? The answers can be found in the following Scripture:

The light shines in the darkness, but the darkness has not understood it (John 1:5).

Once again we must conclude that the issue is not how or when did creation take place, but rather it is a question of God's existence.

This is the verdict: Light has come into the world, but men loved the darkness instead of light because their deeds were evil (John 3:19).

CHAPTER EIGHT

Fifty Years in Search of Nothing

> Yet when I surveyed all that my hands had done and what I had toiled to achieve, everything was meaningless, a chasing after the wind; nothing was gained under the sun (Ecc. 2:11).

The above words were written by a man who realized without God, a lifetime of pursuing knowledge is wasted. There are scientists today who give their whole life in pursuit of an answer that doesn't exist. Their hope is to prove that there is no God. Their entire life's work and devotion will be summed up as "meaningless, a chasing after the wind; nothing was gained under the sun."

Fifty Years in the Lab

Evolutionists are spending an incredible amount of time and effort to prove that life can arise spontaneously from non-living chemicals. While interesting biological chemicals have been produced in the laboratory, no life-generating ones have been produced. One truth glares from these experiments: Evolutionists have *applied a tremendous amount to intelligence* to their experiments in

order to prove life arose *without any intelligence.* Doesn't
it seem peculiar that these brilliant men would spend
fifty years of their life in a lab trying to duplicate life only
to show no intelligence was necessary to form it in the
beginning?

A Closer Look at "Life in the Lab"

In the previous chapter, we briefly stated that Drs.
Stanley Miller and Sidney Fox were famed for their efforts
in attempting to show life could take place spontaneously.
Now we wish to consider a few additional details
regarding their work, which an evolutionary professor will
fail to mention to the students in his classes. To simulate
conditions supposedly corresponding to the imagined
conditions on primitive Earth, Miller and Fox used a
mixture of methane, ammonia and water vapor; then
they passed an electric current through the mixture, and
were able to produce a few amino acids. Did they produce
life? There is no doubt they produced the amino acids
spontaneously, *but not the ones necessary for producing
life.*

Furthermore, the apparatus included a trap to
separate amino acids as soon as they were formed;
otherwise they would have been broken down quickly
and destroyed by the same 'atmospheric' conditions
that produced them. **(See fig. #39.)** Imagine what would
happen if an astronaut decided to step out of his space
suit on the moon. Even if the temperature were a pleasant

Figure 39: A closer look at the apparatus used by Drs. Miller and Fox to synthesize amino acids

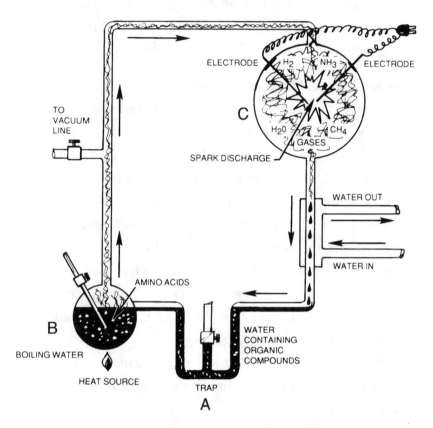

The apparatus for synthesizing amino acids in the laboratory required a trap (A) for the acids after they were formed to isolate them from the energy source; otherwise, the heat (B) and electrical spark (C) etc. would have destroyed them. If life came about by chance, nature would have had to somehow trap these acids. Not likely.

70° F. and he were connected to an oxygen tank, he would be zapped by lethal rays coming from outer space. These are some of the minor problems early, fragile life would have encountered after it had mysteriously appeared. Protection would not have been available on "primitive Earth."

For Miller and Fox's theory to work, the atmosphere would have had to be composed of a swamp gas consisting of deadly carbon monoxide. The theory would strike out before it ever got to first base. Furthermore, the soup of chemicals would have had to be far hotter than the boiling point of water (212° F.) for the raw material to be triggered towards becoming a cell. Such extreme heat would have resulted in its destruction. One evolutionist thought up an idea to compensate for this problem. He suggests the entire scenario took place at the edge of a volcano, and an unexpected rainstorm happened to come along at just the right instant to cool the soup down so the raw materials could continue their journey upward and onward toward becoming life. Data that conflicts with their absurd theory doesn't bother evolutionists; they are making up the rules as they go along. (**See fig. #40.**)

Right-Handed Gloves Don't Fit Left-Handed People

Another fatal flaw exists in Drs. Miller and Fox's experiment. Most amino acids exist in two forms. These are called L (commonly referred to as left-handed) and D

Figure 40: The tale of goo

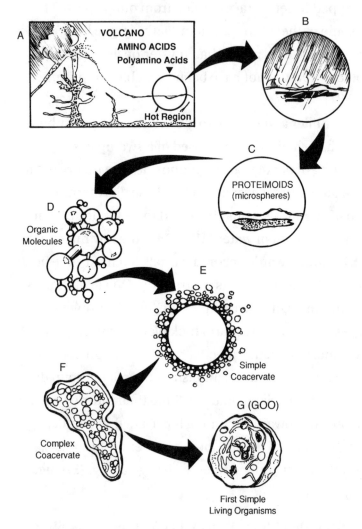

Our evolutionary scenario suggests that life appeared as a result of a series of coincidences in which conditions were suitable for the formation of the first simple one-celled oranism. However, what evolutionists believe came about through blind chance, intelligent man, aided by his sophisticated laboratory equipment, cannot duplicate.

(commonly referred to as right-handed). These two forms
of the same amino acid are alike in that they contain
the same atoms; but the atoms are arranged differently,
making the two acids very distinct.

L and D forms are almost identical, as are two gloves
in a pair, but are not interchangeable. If one needs a
glove to cover his right hand, the left-handed glove
simply will not work, even though it is very similar to a
right-handed glove. Living organisms are assembled only
with left-handed amino acids. Can you imagine a World
Series baseball game in which a left-handed short stop
attempted to play his position with a right-handed glove?
Although he may possibly succeed in doing so, life cannot
succeed — that is, be produced — from right-handed
amino acids. Proteins necessary for life absolutely require
left-handed amino acids.

Now the experiments by Dr. Miller and Dr. Fox which
yielded amino acids always yielded mixtures of the two
forms — both L and D forms instead of only the L form.
To produce the proteins necessary for life, one must
be able to produce amino acids that are exclusively the
"left-handed" type. Neither Miller nor Fox, nor any other
scientist, has been successful in finding the secret to
making the L form alone. **(See fig. # 41.)**

A Lot of Hoopla Over Nothing

Several problems with Drs. Miller and Fox's
experiment have been discussed:

Figure 41: Left and right hand amino acids

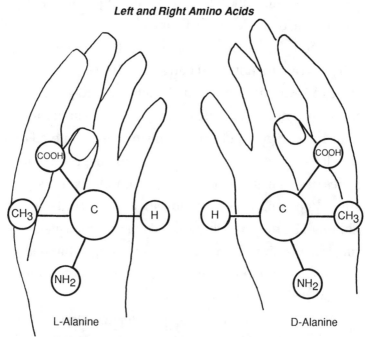

Left and Right Amino Acids

L-Alanine   D-Alanine

Just as a right-handed glove cannot fit on a left hand, neither can the L and D forms of an amino acid be matched, they contain identical atoms.

1. The chemicals used were one million times more concentrated than those found in natural form on Earth.

2. If "the present is the key to the past," and spontaneous generation has never been shown to occur in the lab, then why is it believed to have happened in the past?

3. Pasteur's experiments invalidate the Spontaneous

   Generation Theory.

4. Destructive forces — such as radiation and extreme heat — would have destroyed early, fragile life.

5. The laboratory apparatus included a trap to separate the amino acids as soon as they were formed; otherwise, they would have quickly been destroyed.

6. Fifty years of lab experimentation have not been successful in producing a living cell.

7. Both left-handed and right-handed amino acids, which will not work together to form a living cell, were formed in the experiments.

When Miller and Fox synthesized amino acids in their experiment, it became world news overnight. Since then, there has been a lot of commotion over the fact that scientists can create amino acids in the laboratory. But what's so impressive about getting water to run downhill? Can you imagine a newspaper boy holding up a newspaper and attempting to sell it yelling, "Extra! Extra! Car rolls downhill! Read all about it!" And the cover picture shows a car rolling down hill. Well, that is what happened when Miller and Fox synthesized amino acids in the lab. The only difference was that in the newspapers the wording was changed. Scientific terminology was used, but in reality, the experiment was not much different than getting a car to roll downhill. So it should be no big surprise that these reactions take place quite readily in the laboratory because they do not require outside intelligence. They simply follow the law governing matter — the second law of thermodynamics. On the other hand, getting life to arise spontaneously is an uphill reaction — like getting a car to roll uphill. Such a reaction requires outside intelligence and a reversal of the second law of thermodynamics. If someone does succeed in producing such a reaction in the laboratory, then there would be reason for a lot of hoopla.

The *Scrabble* Game of Life

Producing the uphill reaction that is necessary for life to occur would be like picking the right letters from a *Scrabble* game to write a sentence. Suppose one had *Scrabble* games in English, Chinese, Greek, Hebrew and Arabic with the letter blocks all mixed together. There are many more English letters in the pile than needed for the sentence. Not only is there an excess of letters needed for the sentence, there are some letters — like Q, X and Z — that are totally unusable in the sentence. **(See fig. # 42.)**

Remember Dr. Miller's experiments? He was able to produce different kinds of amino acids — left-handed (L) and right-handed (D) amino acids. Only the "L" can be used. The "D" amino acid cannot be used because it destroys the potential for creating proteins necessary for "creating" life.

And then there are letters in other scripts — Chinese, Greek, Arabic and Hebrew — that must be avoided. These

Figure 42: *The Scrabble game of life*

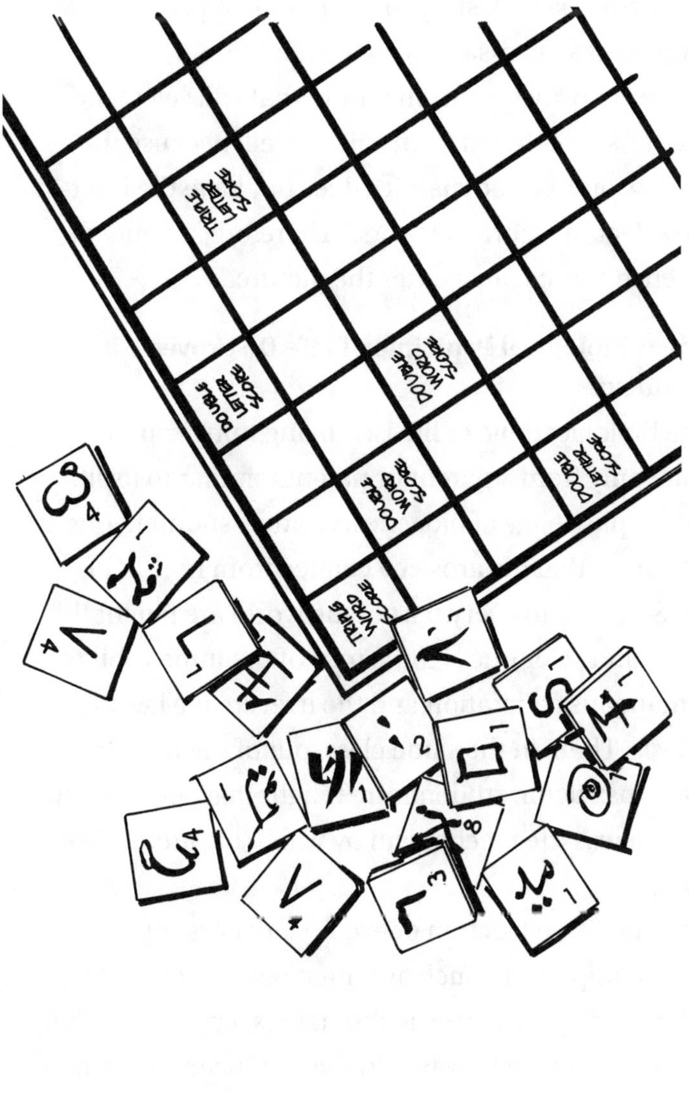

Playing a scrabble game with characters from a variety of languages would be impossible. When amino acids are reproduced in the laboratory, also produced are some other acids. These useless acids destroy the potential for creating the next and much more complex building block of the cell — the protein that is necessary for constructing a cell.

are even more useless than the Q, X and Z. They represent molecules churning about in a "prehistoric primordial soup"; their presence would not only be unnecessary, they would actually destroy the potential to produce the building blocks necessary to create life.

There is no known law in nature that will select the "right letters" needed to form a living cell, because the second law of thermodynamics does not have the built-in laws to select the "correct letters." Therefore, an outside intelligence source must enter the picture.

The Great Biological Principle of Life Disproves Evolutionism

The biological rule of life is: A living thing can originate only from a parent or parents similar to itself. This principle or law of biogenesis refutes spontaneous generation — that life arose by chance from non-living matter. Students in every part of the world are taught the historical and scientific significance of the impossibility of spontaneous generation and the irreversible law of biogenesis. Then, in the same class, out of the mouth of the same instructor, students are taught that spontaneous generation was the mechanism by which life arose. (**See fig. # 43.**)

The rate of destruction of even relatively simple chemical compounds, such as amino acids, by such forces as ultra-violet light or electric discharges, far exceeds their rate of formation. So how would the significant quantities

Figure 43: Meet evolutionist Dr. Hekel and Mr. Hyde

The same evolutionist professors who teach the major biological principle that life comes only from pre-existing life also teach that spontaneous generation was the mechanism by which life arose.

necessary for life to exist ever be produced? This is yet to be satisfactorily answered because it cannot be answered. Lest we forget, the issue is not how or when life began, but whether or not God exists.

> The secret things belong to the LORD our God, but the things revealed belong to us and to our children forever, that we may follow all the words of this law (Deut. 29:29).

The famous astronomer, Sir Fred Hoyle, stated:

Chance of life arising by chance equals 10^{50} blind people each given a *Rubik's Cube,* and all of them solving it at the same time.

CHAPTER NINE

Life Mathematically Impossible Without God

The Spirit of God has made me; the breath of the Almighty gives me life (Job 33:4).

Even a casual look at the hypothesis that life arose by accident reveals its absurdity. And, to complicate matters further, the hypothesis assumes matter is already in existence in some form. The chance hypothesis, then, really only seeks to explain how matter came to be in its present form, and this is not really the question. The primary question is how matter was created from nothing. Nevertheless, let us assume matter *was* already present, and then see if we can answer the question as to whether molecules, compounds, life and so forth, were put together in their present form by a Supreme Intelligence or by blind chance.

Betting on "Poor Ol' Buford"

Although we do not condone betting or gambling in any form, an example of such can be used to illustrate the absurdity of evolutionism's mindless faith that life appeared by blind chance. In fact, gambling and evolutionism go hand-in-hand: They come from the same root. Taking everything into consideration, it has been conservatively calculated that the odds are one chance in $10^{40,000}$ (that is one chance in one followed by 40,000 zeros) that life arose by chance. To give you an idea of the magnitude of these odds, consider the following illustration.

Cover the entire face of the Earth — including the surface of the oceans — with silver dollars, to a depth of about 100 feet. Then color one silver dollar red and let someone hide it anywhere he pleases.

Now blindfold yourself and proceed to select any silver dollar. You may take as long as you wish; but you will have only one chance to select the red silver dollar. What do you suppose the odds are that you will select the red silver dollar? But this illustration does not give you an accurate picture; the number of silver dollars we used is not even one percent of the actual odds necessary for life to have arisen by chance.

For scientists to accept these mind-boggling odds is not science, but the most absurd gamble of all times. To do so would be like saying, "Even though I know the odds for my ten-year-old horse, poor Buford **(see fig. #44)** who has never run a race before, to win the Kentucky Derby are one chance in 10 billion (which doesn't come close to one chance in $10^{40,000}$); I'm going to bet my entire life's savings on him. I'm betting that all the other horses will

Figure 44: Poor ol' Buford

Poor ol' Buford — his owner believes he is a race horse.

die during the race by some freak accident, or that all
the other entries will be unable to finish the race except
mine." Reason is not a part of this scenario, but rather
mindless deception. One willing to believe against such
odds is walking in darkness.

> This is the verdict: Light has come into the world,
> but men loved darkness instead of light because
> their deeds were evil (John 3:19).
>
> … All will be condemned who have not believed
> the truth but have delighted in wickedness (II
> Thess. 2:12).

Only a fool would say, "The evidence says otherwise; so I don't know how it happened, but it did." The fool is one who doesn't believe in God (Psa. 53:1). One who doesn't believe in God has no wisdom, for the beginning of wisdom starts with believing in Him (Prov. 1:7). No wonder people bet on such inconceivable odds. They lack wisdom. But remember that the issue is not how and when life originated; rather, it is how to avoid the Author of truth and righteousness — God.

The Protein Molecule

The protein molecule is a very large one. It is a building block of the cell's computer, the DNA molecule, which is considered the starting place of life. The protein molecule is made up of only five of the 92 elements known to occur naturally in the Earth: carbon, hydrogen, oxygen, sulfur and nitrogen. Proteins are not alive; they are simply the building blocks of the living cell. Just like the bricks of a house are not the house, but simply the building blocks of a house. The simplest cell contains 239 proteins. Each protein is a very complex building block in itself.

What would the odds be of a protein molecule being formed by chance? (For five atoms out of 92 to combine in multiple numbers to produce a protein molecule?) A renowned Swiss mathematician, Charles Eugene Guye, has calculated the odds are one in 10^{160}. (In other words, one chance in one with 160 zeros after it.) These are

Figure 45: Poor ol' crippled Buford

Poor ol' Buford has been crippled since birth.

the odds that one simple little protein molecule could
have come about by chance. That is not even taking into
consideration that it would have had to react with many
other molecules to eventually form a DNA molecule
— the starting point of life. *Remember, one in 10^{160} is
a number larger than all of the electrons in the entire
universe (10^{131} power).*

The odds for poor old Buford to win the race look
bleak. Yet evolutionism is demanding that we bet on
old Buford — that is, that life arose spontaneously even
though the odds for winning are totally absurd.

The Time Element

How long would it take for one protein molecule to be formed by chance? Thus far, we have only been concerned with the odds for one protein molecule to be formed by chance. Now we shall consider the time necessary for a protein to form by chance, and we are still light years away from life. Dr. Guye's calculations indicate it would take 10^{243} years (or one with 243 zeros after it) for one protein molecule to form by chance. This number is so large it would take six lines on this page just to type the number of zeros. According to the evolutionary theory, a most liberal estimate of the Earth's age is six billion years (6,000,000,000). Compare this with the length of time it would take a protein molecule to be formed by chance. It is obvious: Life is mathematically impossible — unless there is a Supreme Intelligence to direct its formation! Poor Buford not only is ten years old and never won a race, but has one broken leg. **(See fig. #45.)**

Additional Difficulties

Dr. J. B. Leathes, an English biologist, has also calculated the number of different ways the atoms in a protein molecule can be arranged by chance. This number turns out to be 10^{48}. Once again we see the chances of getting the right combination necessary to create life is so small, mathematics demands that intelligence must be involved and the materials needed supplied. Poor Buford not only has a broken leg, but he is

Figure 46: Poor ol' crippled, blind Buford

Poor ol' Buford was born crippled and blind.

blind. **(See fig. #46.)**

Calculations Based on Ideal Conditions

All of these calculations have been made by experts in the field, and all have assumed ideal conditions. Yet the environment on early Earth is thought by evolutionists to have been deadly. How life could survive on Earth in its infancy under such conditions is another problem not surmounted by advocates of the theory of evolutionism. Realizing the incredible delicacy of the materials used to create life, it becomes apparent life did not begin by chance, but by the careful design and direction of a Supreme Being.

DNA

Now we shall advance from simple arithmetic to more advanced mathematics. After calculating the mathematical odds and time required for production of a protein, a building block of the DNA molecule, we shall now tackle the immense mathematical odds for the development of the DNA molecule to happen by chance.

Figure 47: The DNA molecule

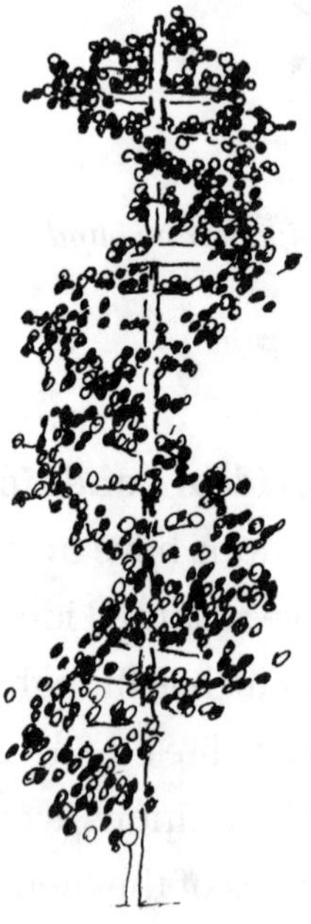

Resembling a spiral staircase, the DNA molecule is a machine with 100 billion moving parts (atoms); it resides within the nucleus of the cell.

Figure 48: The fate of poor ol' Buford

As previously mentioned, the difference in the complexity of the DNA molecule and a protein could be compared to the difference between a child's paper airplane and a U.S. space shuttle. **(See fig. #47.)**

I'm afraid we will find that our potential race horse, poor Buford, not only is 10 years old, has never won a race, has a broken leg and is blind, but that he has been dead for many years. **(See fig. #48.)**

Biologists today are greatly interested in a very complicated molecule called the "deoxyribonucleic acid" molecule, or DNA for short. Science has learned a great deal about life and how it is developed, maintained and regenerated. It is now a well-established fact that the basic starting place for life is the DNA molecule. The DNA molecule is perhaps the most important substance in a cell. DNA is the language in the heart of a cell; it comes complete with a set of instructions telling the cell how to construct itself and run the program, like the software that runs a computer.

DNA was only recently seen directly for the first time. Scientists used a device called an electron-tunneling microscope. This microscope, said to be capable of "seeing" an individual atom, magnifies 1,000,000 times — as opposed to a standard electron microscope which magnifies 300,000 times; a conventional microscope using light can only magnify 1,000 times. The image produced is a computer-generated one resulting from the "viewing" of the electron-tunneling microscope.[14] **(See fig. #49.)**

The DNA molecule resembles a spiral staircase. It is a machine with 100 billion moving parts called atoms. There are as many atoms in one molecule of DNA as there are stars in a typical galaxy. DNA controls our genetic makeup and the very formation of our bodies. This huge molecule determines whether one is an ant or an anteater, a banana or a banana-eating ape, slimy goo or gooing baby. How does the DNA determine what one will be?

The DNA molecule is a cell's computer that has been programmed with blueprint information written in the

Figure 49: The language of the DNA molecule

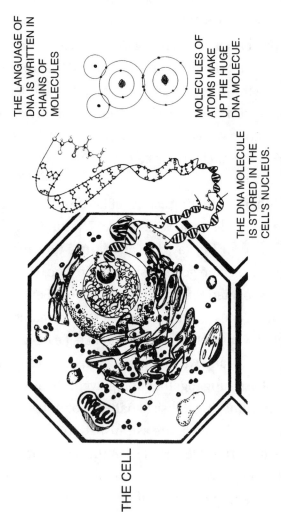

THE LANGUAGE OF DNA IS WRITTEN IN CHAINS OF MOLECULES

MOLECULES OF ATOMS MAKE UP THE HUGE DNA MOLECUE.

THE DNA MOLECULE IS STORED IN THE CELL'S NUCLEUS.

THE CELL

Biochemists estimate there are 10^{87} (1 with 87 zeros after it) ways to assemble the material in just one tiny cross section (A) of DNA.

language of chemistry. This information would fill 1,000 large books, each with 500 pages of small, single-spaced print. It is written down in a chemical code similar to the Morse Code (e.g. SOS ... — — — ...). It is this information which prescribes how a living organism is made and how it is maintained. A teaspoonful of DNA is estimated to have an information capacity equal to a modern computer with a volume of 100 cubic miles. There is a genetic code stored or written in the DNA molecule located in the nucleus of a cell. **(See fig. #50.)**

Music in Genes

Another fascinating aspect of DNA was recently discovered. It has to do with music. The kind of person who likes music but says he can't carry a tune may be wrong. A respected geneticist, Susumo Ono, claims that he has discovered music in human genes, fish genes and rabbit genes. Susumo Ono is a DNA researcher. He wondered what DNA would sound like if each chemical on the DNA strand was assigned a musical note and those notes strung together and played. He discovered something amazing: Musical patterns of notes that reveal intelligence. Musicians are astonished to hear echoes of Bach, Schubert or Mozart in DNA music. Using the same formula for converting DNA into music, Dr. Ono worked backwards and translated Chopin's funeral march into chemical symbols. It came out *cancer!* Skeptics point out these strings of DNA produce only a string of single notes; it is the musicians who fill in the rhythm and the

Figure 50: The library of DNA

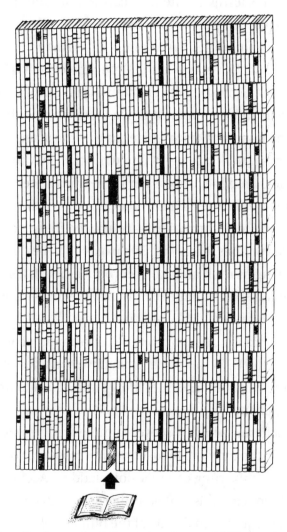

The DNA molecule contains information that would fill 1,000 large volumes, each with 500 pages.

harmony. But any way one looks at it, the patterns of single notes testify to intelligence and not a blind random force in nature as the source of DNA.[15]

Bell Laboratories have done studies on the mathematical language in the DNA molecule and have found that its mathematical pattern is identical to that of conversational language. Since there is no doubt in anyone's mind it takes intelligence to write a language, it is obvious it took intelligence to write the DNA code.

One incredible process performed by the cell is the formation of new cells. This process requires the entire DNA library of information — contained in the equivalent of 1,000 volumes, each with 500 pages — to be duplicated. The cell reads itself and then reproduces itself; it does the duplication in about 20 minutes. Try that — and do it without mistakes.

How did this mass of complex information come to reside in the DNA molecule? And, if we consider DNA to be the starting point of "life," how difficult is it to produce DNA by chance?

Biochemists have discovered there are 10^{87} ways to assemble the material in just one tiny cross section of the DNA. (Like one rung of a mile-long ladder.) According to evolutionism, this fantastically complicated molecule — which is just a small part of the human cell — came into existence by time and chance, by trial and error. The problem with this is that there is only one combination out of the 10^{87} ways that will work for reproduction. Now

10^{87} is a one with 87 zeros after it; and there are only 10^{17} number of seconds in 10 billion years — the time given by the evolutionists for the age of the universe. That's like having a giant jigsaw puzzle comprised of one followed by 87 zeros number of pieces, yet one has to put five pieces of the puzzle together every second to complete it in 10 billion years, the amount of time evolutionists say the universe may have taken to come into existence. Furthermore, one has to put the puzzle together blindfolded. That's incredibly absurd. Even if a trial and error method were attempted once every second, there would not have been nearly enough time to bring together just one "rung" (tiny step) of DNA in the amount of time evolutionists say the Earth has existed. **(See fig. #51.)**

The Question Remains: Where did DNA get the Information?

Again we come back to the question of how the blueprint information arrived in the DNA molecule in the first place. The pure chemistry of a cell is not sufficient to explain the workings of a cell, although the workings are chemical. For example, the physics and the chemistry of a watch can explain its function, but they cannot explain its origin.

Did DNA get its information from the laws of the chemicals? No. Chemicals have laws, but do not direct a language or message that makes sense. When considering

Figure 51: The chances of chance producing DNA

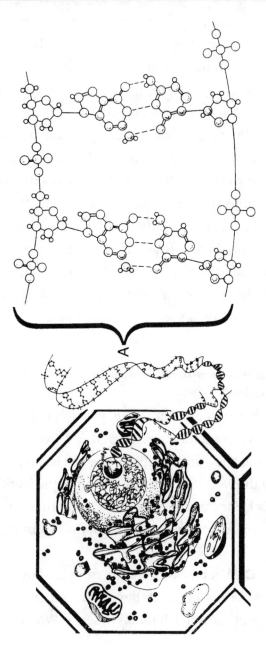

Biochemists estimate there are 10^{87} (1 with 87 zeros after it) ways to assemble the material in just one tiny cross section (A) of DNA.

the natural forces of nature verses intelligent forces from a human being, we see the problem more clearly. By intelligent forces we mean the ability to write a book, program a computer or compose a symphony. We know that natural laws only reproduce geometric patterns, as in the formation of sand ripples, crystal or ferns. Here the natural laws do nothing more than to pick a shape and order it to be made again and again and again.

We see the difference between natural forces and intelligent forces when comparing a beautiful stone with an arrowhead or by comparing a beautiful cave formation with Mount Rushmore. In nature, the difference is evident because the formations we see in clouds or sand are beautiful, but random. However, if we were to see a formation in the clouds or sand that read, 'John loves Mary,' we would know that random forces did not make this, but rather intelligent forces.

In 1967, astronomers detected radio signals coming from outer space and labeled them LGM. They thought maybe there was intelligence out there trying to communicate with us. LGM stands for "Little Green Men." However, study revealed the signals were the wrong kind of language. It was discovered to be a pulsar star that mimics a radio beacon.

DNA has too much information, information that requires an intelligent agent to create it and write out the language. The chemical workings of a cell are controlled by the blueprint information that does not reside in the atoms and molecules of a cell. Therefore, there must be an Author (God) Who transcends the material, the matter of which the DNA molecule is made.

This Author, first of all, conceived the information necessary to make a cell; secondly, He wrote it down in the cell; thirdly, He devised a mechanism by which the cell could read itself; fourthly, He devised a mechanism by which the cell could build or reproduce itself; and lastly, He devised a mechanism by which the cell could maintain itself. To say all this is the result of blind chance is ridiculous.

The Equation for Life

Laboratory experiments have served one purpose: They clearly show it takes intelligence and controlled planning to manufacture even the simplest of building materials for living organisms. Rather than confirming the idea of life arising from non-living materials, experiments have proven the necessity of intelligence and planning for the origin of life. Life is mathematically impossible without God. Here is the equation for the origin of life:

The POWER of God + The CREATIVITY of God + The INTELLIGENCE of God = LIFE

It appears that poor Buford was never alive. Poor Buford is nothing more than a figment of an overactive imagination. It is a blind, humanistic notion concocted over 100 years ago. It never did have a leg to stand on, let alone a broken leg.

Examining the roots of evolutionism, it becomes easy to see that it was concocted by men who had rejected God.

> For although they knew God, they neither glorified him as God nor gave thanks to him, but their thinking became futile and their foolish hearts were darkened. Although they claimed to be wise, they became fools and exchanged the glory of the immortal God for images made to look like mortal man and birds and animals and reptiles (Rom. 1:21-23).

CHAPTER TEN

Spontaneous "Excalibur" Combustion

A fool's mouth is his undoing, and his lips are a snare to his soul (Prov. 18:7).

Who ever heard of a robot creating itself? Science fiction writers have written some incredible sagas and the motion picture industry has produced movies of fantasy; but in reality, robots do not create themselves.

Who ever heard of the laws of physics, which govern the atoms of various elements — such as steel, rubber, glass, plastic — designing and producing an "Excalibur" automobile? No one has! Why not? Because the blueprint for the car is not contained within the atoms of the materials of which it is made. There is no instructive urge within steel, glass, rubber or plastic causing them to be shaped into doors, windows, wheels and an engine. Something beyond the materials of the "Excalibur" is required to dictate a blueprint, a design. Something outside the laws of physics and chemistry determines the conditions under which physical objects come into existence. **(See fig. #52.)**

Figure 52: The Excalibur — Masterpiece of artistic engineering

Who would believe the laws of physcics governing the atoms of elements such as steel, rubber, glass and plastic would also design and produce an Excalibur automobile? It is obvious to everyone that something outside the laws of physics determines the conditions under which physical objects come into existence

Evolutionists attempt to use the operational laws of physics to prove their theories for both the origin of the universe and the origin of life. It is as if one is watching a video played in reverse; an automobile blown apart by a box of dynamite suddenly reassembles itself. This represents what evolutionism has proposed. Add several billion years to the initial few seconds of the "Big Bang" explosion, and the pieces of the car slowly come together.

The operational laws governing the universe cannot and must not be used to try to explain the origins of the universe. Likewise, the laws governing matter cannot be used to explain the origin and creation of life. To do so is like saying the laws governing the atoms of the various parts of a watch can be used to explain and determine the origins of the watch.

Evolutionists insist the physical/chemical laws in operation today can explain the origin of life. In other words, everything that occurred in the past is assumed to be explainable by the physical/chemical laws at work in the world today.

Creationists disagree. They argue that although natural laws may be adequate to explain how things function today, they are not capable of explaining how they arrived in the first place. There is nothing about an "Excalibur" automobile that contradicts the laws of chemistry and physics. Each part functions in complete harmony with all the laws normally governing matter and energy. Yet matter and energy, each on their own, could never produce an "Excalibur" spontaneously.

The same reasoning applies to the origin of life. One can use the laws of physics and chemistry to describe how living things function, but these laws do not explain how life came into being. There is no spontaneous urge within the raw materials of nature to develop and become living systems.

Refusing to accept even the possibility of a Creator, evolutionists can only conceive that living creatures can be completely reduced to the laws of physics and chemistry which governed atoms and molecules for their existence — no more, no less.

Imagine for a Moment …

For a moment, let us suppose the evolutionist is correct regarding the laws of physics and chemistry governing atoms and molecules. Let us try to imagine that an "Excalibur" could have risen by some set of unusual circumstances wherein the laws governing the atoms and molecules of glass, rubber and steel did, in fact, produce the automobile. Let us try to imagine that life could have risen from the laws governing the atoms and molecules of matter.

Let's consider the evolutionary claim, "The present is the key to the past" on its own terms. What laws were operating when life appeared on planet Earth? If life arose from a soup of chemicals, as evolutionism proposes, then these chemicals were subject to the same physical laws and processes we see at work in the world today. One of the laws in operation today is known as the second law of thermodynamics. This law totally destroys the possibility of life arising from non-living substances.

The Second Law of Thermodynamics

The second law of thermodynamics states that all energy is running in a downward trend. In other words, matter is moving from an organized structure to a disorganized state. Natural processes, left alone, tend toward disorder and disarray. Just allowing one's room to go unattended for a month demonstrates this principle in action very clearly! **(See fig. #53.)**

Figure 53: The Second Law of thermodynamics

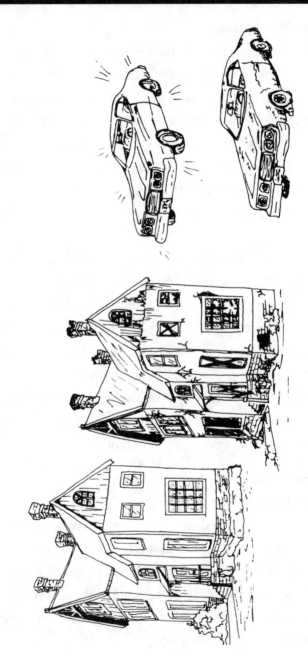

The second law of thermodynamics states that the universe is moving from an organized condition to a disorganized one, which positively refutes the theory of evolutionism.

As time passes, what was once organized, intelligible data becomes more and more garbled, unintelligible, disorganized data. Time results in the loss of intelligent information, not in its accumulation. The second law of thermodynamics contradicts the evolutionary claim that at the origin of life, chemicals tended spontaneously toward higher order and complexity.

The second law of thermodynamics utterly destroys the idea of spontaneous "Excalibur" combustion. The car would rust, decay and fall apart long before enough time would pass in order for the parts to become somehow shaped, produced and assembled by the physical laws governing atoms and molecules.

In real life, things don't go from worse to better, but from better to worse. The laws of science flatly contradict the theory of evolutionism that the simple becomes more complex in time. This is a fairy tale that many adults have accepted as truth.

> They exchanged the truth of God for a lie, and worshiped and served created things rather than the Creator ... (Rom. 1:25).

Evolved Parts?

Years ago, I had the privilege of attending L'Abri, in Switzerland, founded by the late Christian apologist, Francis Schaeffer. I heard Schaeffer use an argument against evolutionism that was simple, easy to understand and devastating. He explained, "Suppose a fish evolves lungs. What happens then? Does it move up to the next evolutionary stage? Of course not. It drowns."

In other words, living things cannot simply change piecemeal by somehow acquiring a new organ here and a new limb there. An organism is an extremely integrated system. If there is any isolated change in the system, it is more likely to be harmful than helpful. For example, if a fish's gills were to begin mutating so that they could change into a set of lungs, it would be a disaster, not an advantage. The only way to turn a fish into a land-dwelling animal is to transform it all at once, with a host of interrelated changes happening all at the same time. Not only must the lungs develop, there must be changes in the skeleton, the circulatory system and all the other dozen parts and systems.

Consider the mousetrap. **(See fig. #54.)** It cannot be assembled gradually and at the same time be fully functional. You cannot start with a wooden platform and catch a mouse, add a spring and catch another mouse, followed by adding a hammer, and so on. In order to catch mice, all the parts must be assembled from the outset. The mousetrap will not work until all its parts are present and working together.

Likewise, living creatures are similar to the mousetrap. They are made up of an entire system of interacting parts all working together. If one part is not there, the entire system of interacting parts will not function. Keep in mind that according to Darwinism,

Figure 54: The mousetrap

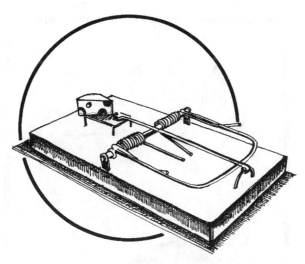

The mousetrap will not work until all its parts are present and working together..

natural selection preserves the forms that function better than their rivals. All the non-functioning systems are eliminated by natural selection, such as in the case of a fish evolving lungs. There is no possible Darwinian explanation as to how these complex structures and systems came into existence.

A classic example of this principle is found in the human eye, which can differentiate 1,000 shades of color **(See fig. #55.)** An eye is of no use at all unless all its parts are fully formed and working together. Even a slight variation from its present form destroys its function and purpose. How it could be possible for the eye to slowly

Figure 55: The Eye

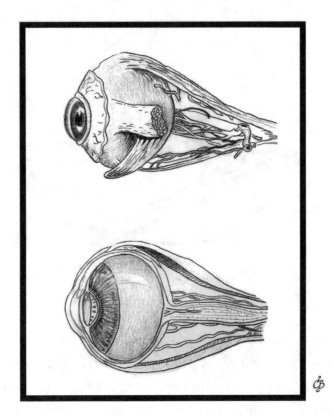

An eye is of no use at all unless all its parts are fully formed and working together.

evolve is a question even Darwin couldn't explain. Even in Darwin's day, the complexity of the eye was used as evidence against his theory, and Darwin said the mere thought of trying to explain the eye gave him "a cold shudder."

The most advanced, automated, modern, computerized lens of a camera is light- years less in complexity than the human eye. The mutations (changes) required to produce complex organs, such as an eye or a bird's wing — not to mention the thousands of other organs — could never have occurred in a series of tiny mutations accumulating over thousands of generations. The individual parts of the organs are useless and of no advantage to a living creature, unless the entire organ is functioning. The hundreds of parts needed for an eye, or a bird's wing, to work, all have to be there, or the other parts are useless and serve no advantage. The mathematical probability of hundreds of such random mutations happening together in one generation is zero. This is why many evolutionists have escaped to the realm of fantasy by adapting the theory of punctuated equilibrium. This irrational theory suggests that a new species could appear suddenly, with no traces of the slow transformation that Darwin promoted. An example of this absurd theory suggests that when a dinosaur laid its brood of a dozen eggs, all of them hatched as normal little dino-babies with one exception. One may have hatched into a fully functioning bird, feathers, wings and all. It mutated so fast that it somehow became a fully functional and totally different species. How is that for legitimate science? This is nothing more than an adult fairy tale.

The reason for this wild notion is that ever since Charles Darwin first published his *Origin of the Species*

promoting natural selection in 1859, there have been
challenges to his theory, not only by Christians, but by
evolutionary non-Christians as well. Moderate critics
are producing increasingly devastating critiques against
the evolutionary theory. After more than 100 years of
experimental breeding of various kinds of animals and
plants, the amount of variation that can be produced,
even with intentional (not random) breeding, is extremely
limited, and can only proceed to the limited range of
genetic variation within each type of living thing. In
other words, one can breed dogs to look like everything
between a tiny Pekinese and a Saint Bernard, but all of
them will still be dogs. You can't go beyond a certain
limit. The outcome of selectively-controlled breeding for
generations is still the same species. Birds are still birds,
dogs are still dogs, fruit flies are still fruit flies and so
forth. In the last 130 years of intense archeological activity
— beginning with Darwin's time — the evolutionary
community has failed to procure even one convincing
example of an intermediate or transitional type of fossil,
showing some characteristic of developmental progress,
in or toward evolutionism. Nothing has been found that
would be necessary to fill in the gaps of the fossil record
between distinct kinds of animals and those alive today.
Advances in molecular biology increasingly reveal the
incredible complexity of even the simplest of organisms,
with no satisfactory explanation for the origin of those
differences given.

CHAPTER ELEVEN

A Monkey Tale

Words from a wise man's mouth are gracious, but a fool is consumed by his own lips. At the beginning his words are folly; at the end they are wicked madness (Ecc. 10:12-13).

Have you ever heard of a monkey typing? Whoever heard of a monkey that not only can type, but is able to produce a famous classic such as Shakespeare's "Hamlet"?

The Planet of the Monkeys

Evolutionists proclaim: "Given enough time, anything might be possible." Yes, it's true; even if one experimented with a room full of monkeys, all sitting at computers, given enough time, one monkey might accidentally produce an intelligent three-letter word like "pop." This is what the evolutionary theory proposes: Given enough time, unintelligent forces might, by chance, produce some intelligent information, which might give rise to more intelligence. Maybe a second monkey might come along, in time, and accidentally type "lolly" in front of "pop," so we have an increase in accidental knowledge. Now we

Figure 56: The tale of a monkey

have "lollypop." **(See fig. #56.)**

How did the computer backspace so that "lolly" could be typed before "pop"? What evolutionism is really teaching is that the second law of thermodynamics would have had to be operating in reverse in order for evolutionism to take place. **(See fig. #57.)**

The evolutionary theory then proceeds from the ridiculous to the absurd. It is one thing to think a room full of monkeys at computers might eventually come up with the word "lollypop," but what are the chances they would compose the 20 million volumes-worth of intelligent information representing man? That is like believing after 100 million generations of random chance, the word "lollypop" could somehow evolve into a brilliant classic, such as Shakespeare's "Hamlet." In order to produce "Hamlet," a group of monkeys would have to hit certain keys randomly, as evolutionism asserts, 15 quadrillion times in succession *without making a mistake.*

The second law of thermodynamics destroys any potential that chance can produce order and complexity. Evolutionists attempt to counter the argument that creationists use regarding the second law of thermodynamics by claiming that the processes taking place at the origin of life were not "left to themselves" (that is, were not left to the second law of thermodynamics). Rather, the Earth was open to the sun's energy, which would offset the natural tendency toward disorder. In other words, the monkeys weren't

Figure 57: "Give me time," cries the evolutionist

left to themselves but they had some outside help — not intelligent help, but orderly help. This outside help was another law of physics in operation, which supposedly, somehow reversed the second law of thermodynamics.

Just how valid is this evolutionary rebuttal? First of all, have you ever heard of a law without a lawgiver? "Well, of course," replies the evolutionist, especially when it comes to moral laws which have eternal consequences attached to them such as the Ten Commandments.

Perpetual Motion Machines

For centuries, men of science have attempted to invent some contraption that would offset the second law of thermodynamics. They have failed in every attempt. Evolutionists are still proclaiming that somehow, at some time, in the past, the second law of thermodynamics was overcome; non-living matter reversed the law and caused itself to become living matter.

In the article, "Perpetual Motion Machines,"[16] Stanley Angrist provides a host of ingenious proposals — all doomed by the law of thermodynamics. Although the article does not mention evolutionism, it does discuss other failed efforts in the history of science to devise mechanisms attempting to conquer the second law of thermodynamics, as evolutionism claims to do.

$1,000 Reward

The Bradbury Engineered Solutions offers $1,000 to any school providing any "scientific" evidence whatsoever that "first life" arose spontaneously. ... Or proof that changes between basic animal species (as from invertebrates to vertebrates, fish to amphibian, amphibian to reptile, etc.) has ever evolved.

$5,000 Cash Reward

R. G. Elmendorf offers a $5,000 cash reward for anyone who can find a natural process in which available energy, structure and information increase with time, without requiring prior and higher energy, structure and information. Evolutionists claim this is what happened at the outset of life, but so far no one has collected the $5,000 reward for the proof.

$250 Grand

Well-known creationist Kent Hovind offers anyone $250,000 who can prove evolutionism as evidence for creation.

The second law of thermodynamics is referred to in the Bible. It is the curse in Scripture, which became effective at the time of Adam and Eve's sin (Gen. 3), and has resulted in death and decay throughout the entire universe.

Back to the Planet of the Monkeys

Any intelligence, that might have accidentally arisen, would have been adversely affected — not only by the second law of thermodynamics, but also by other unintelligent and destructive forces. For example, what about the other 99 monkeys in our tale? Although one or two might accidentally type an intelligent word, the other 99 would be about their normal monkey business of remodeling the room and each other. This is exactly what would have happened had life suddenly appeared on the horizon. It would have entered a hostile and lethal environment, which would have immediately destroyed it.

The evolutionary theory is full of occurrences that can only be labeled miraculous, and were supposedly brought about by unintelligent forces. It certainly demands blind faith to believe spontaneous life could have occurred, let alone could have continued its existence, in an environment that included nothing necessary to its survival. It would have taken a carload of miracles for life to advance up the tree of complexity, defying the laws of thermodynamics. It is amazing how a drowning man will try to save himself, grasping at anything. A man who rejects God will go to great lengths to avoid, rather than face, the One Who reveals the evil and wickedness in his heart.

CHAPTER TWELVE

The "Uphill" Mystery of Life: Teleonomy

> Jesus answered, "I am the way and the truth and the life. No one comes to the Father except through me" (John 14:6).

What is this mysterious, intelligent energy causing life to flow uphill, offsetting, for a time, the natural tendency towards disorder described in the second law of thermodynamics?

Scientists have found that all living things have within their structure a mysterious, built-in machine which captures energy and transforms it for its own use. Non-living things do not have this mechanism, and scientists do not know exactly what it is, how it works or from where it came; they only know it exists. They have named it teleonomy.

A living flower, by means of a "secret" process, teleonomy, is capable of using the sun's energy to advance complexity and to sustain its life — though eventually it will fall prey to the second law of thermodynamics (death). If the flower is picked, it immediately dies, and the sun's rays serve only to hasten it decay. Teleonomy, then, is some sort of built-in factory (system) that transforms energy into order. Without it, energy is either useless or destructive.

As previously mentioned, the DNA molecule is perhaps the most important substance in a cell. It has enough blueprint information written in the language of chemistry to fill 1,000 large books, each with 500 pages of small single-spaced print — information which describes how to make man and how to maintain him. A teaspoonful of DNA is estimated to have an information capacity equal to a modern computer with a volume of 100 cubic miles. But how in the world did this information come to reside in the DNA molecule?

Energy + Matter + Outside Information = Life

The pure chemistry of a cell is not sufficient to explain the workings of a cell, although the workings are chemical. As previously mentioned, physics and chemistry can explain the function of a watch, but cannot explain its origin. The chemical workings of a cell are controlled by information that does not reside in the atoms and molecules of the cell. Therefore, there must be an Author (God) Who transcends the material — the matter of which the DNA molecule is made.

Requirement for All "Uphill" Living Machines

All living systems — such as plants, animals and man

— require three things in order to operate:
  1) an appropriate source of energy;
  2) a structure or mechanism capable of converting the energy for use; and
  3) an intelligent information and control system to direct the conversion mechanism.

For example, an automobile (inanimate) has an engine capable of converting fuel into useful energy. But it doesn't have the ability to create itself; it needs outside intelligence (man) to build it, make it work and maintain it. Only living things have the necessary three components for life. Where did living organisms acquire this self-reproducing, self-starting, self-directing, self-repairing and self-maintaining mechanism? From unintelligent, random processes and chance — or an intelligent source called Creator God?

Odds for Evolutionism

One of the most well-known evolutionists, Julian Huxley, estimated the probability of natural selection (a law of nature) leading to higher forms (such as ape to man) is one chance in a number so large it would occupy 1,500 pages of print. Then he makes another statement, which reveals the amazing depth of his anti-God zeal:

> No one would bet on anything so improbable happening. ... And yet it happened.[17]

Believing in the evolutionary theory, then, is taking

the greatest gamble of all time — a gamble bordering on the absurd. But then again, the issue is not how and when life began, but rather whether or not God can exist. For the atheistic evolutionist, the answer is, "Of course not."

The problem is not that truth cannot be found, but rather that truth is not loved.

> This is the verdict: Light has come into the world, but men loved darkness instead of light because their deeds were evil (John 3:19).

CHAPTER THIRTEEN

The Evidence of an Intelligent Creation

By wisdom the LORD laid the earth's foundations, by understanding he set the heavens in place (Prov. 3:19).

Evidence of an Intelligent Creator

In 1993, a group of prestigious scientists and researchers gathered to discuss their shared dissatisfaction with the accepted explanation of natural selection as an answer to the question of the origins of life. As they considered the empirical evidence of their combined understanding of molecular biology, chemistry and genetics, they came to the following conclusions concerning the decades-long debate over natural selection versus intelligent design. The laws of chemistry and physics cannot explain the origins and complexity of life, therefore there must be some kind of intelligence and guiding hand in the process of life and the origins of living systems. The information in this chapter reveals why these distinguished and eminent scholars came to such a conclusion.

Most evolutionists proclaim that the biblical account
of creation doesn't belong in the science classroom
because one can't observe it. Even some Christians
wonder if it's really possible to find positive, scientific
evidence of intelligence behind creation, even though
proof can be found easily and naturally in the normal
course of everyday events.

Suppose, for example, a person is strolling down
a creek bed. Once in awhile, he picks up a pebble with
some interesting shape, perhaps one that reminds him
of a face or a picture. Although these objects have some
appearance of design, they are really only what would be
expected from time, chance and the natural processes of
weathering and erosion.

Figure 58: Produced by chance?

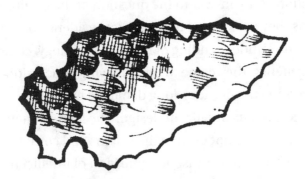

*Even if one had no previous knowledge of Indian artifacts, an
arrowhead among the rocks and pebbles in a creek would immediately
stand out as an object produced by someone for a purpose. It is not
difficult to recognize the evidence of intelligent creation.*

Indian Artifact

But suppose he then comes across an Indian arrowhead or stone trinket among the pebbles. Even if he had no previous knowledge of Indian artifacts, the object would immediately stand out as distinct and unique. **(See fig. #58.)** The difference would be spotted easily, for it would be obvious that time, chance and erosion would never produce such a shape. The person would instantly recognize this object was produced with a purpose in mind; without seeing either the creator or the creative act, it would be simple to recognize evidence of an intelligent creation. Thus, in our everyday experience, we regularly distinguish between two classes of objects: (1) objects created with or for a purpose; and (2) those resulting from time, chance and various natural processes.

Astronomers and government officials are spending billions of dollars in a search for intelligent life in outer space; they are convinced they would be able to tell the difference between signal patterns produced by chance and those sent out with deliberate intent. Their belief serves to support the creationists' viewpoint; it is easy to discern the difference between design by intelligence and those things that come about by random processes.

The Snowflake

The distinguishable difference between things which come about through an intelligent process and those which come about through random processes is not

Figure 59: The snowflake

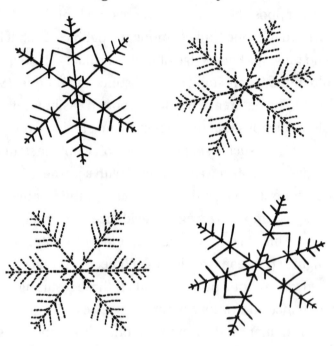

"design" per se, but the kind of design. A snowflake, for example, may have an incredibly beautiful pattern and appear quite complex, yet each snowflake results from water molecules doing what comes naturally under certain conditions. **(See fig. #59.)** A tile mosaic made in a snowflake pattern has no greater evidence of design, yet we recognize it as a pattern created by intelligence. Why? Because we know bits of colored stone do not arrange themselves in such patterns. Such a work of art must be produced by an intelligent source. Thus man can distinguish created objects on the basis of scientific observation and logical conclusion.

Natural Forces or Intelligent Forces

   It is an accepted fact, that natural forces produce
non-complex or redundant form, while intelligent forces
produce complex design and pattern. The difference
is, one conveys intelligent information and the other
does not. Random forces do not produce intelligent

Figure 60: Intelligent design is obvious

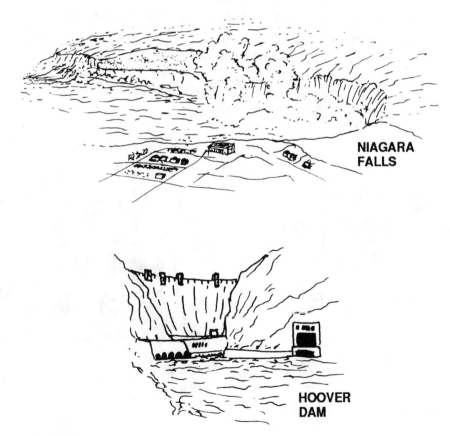

NIAGARA
FALLS

HOOVER
DAM

information; only intelligent forces can produce intelligent information. As breathtaking as Niagara Falls is, when we look at it, we think in terms of "natural" phenomenon, but when we see Hoover Dam, we recognize intelligence and design with a purpose behind the construction. **(See fig. #60.)** We think of a crystal rock as being formed by nature, but we immediately understand that conception, design and craftsmanship were used as we gaze admiringly at a chandelier. **(See fig. #61.)** The same can be said of cloud formations on a summer afternoon; we would conclude that a natural force of nature has produced the formations. However,

Figure 61: Design with a purpose is apparent

CHANDELIER

ROCK CRYSTAL

Figure 62: Intelligent forces versus chance

Seeing one's name spelled out in a cloud formation, one immediately recognizes that it is not the product of blind chance, but that intelligent forces were involved.

if we were to see our names spelled out in the cloud formation, we would know this was not the product of blind chance; but rather, intelligent forces were involved. **(See fig. # 62.)**

Mount Rushmore

In the Black Hills of South Dakota there stands a national monument. If a person has never seen nor heard of Mt. Rushmore and suddenly came upon it while hiking through the wilderness, at once he would conclude that the elements of nature did not fashion the rock into four monoliths with the faces of men, but that intelligence was involved. Millions of years of wind and water erosion would never form replicas of the presidents' heads. Only the feebleminded would be unable to recognize the intellect, purpose, design and sculpturing abilities involved in such a masterpiece. **(See fig. #63.)**

Figure 63: Intelligent forccces or chance?

The Mount Rushmore National Monument

Living Systems

Now when we turn our attention to life and focus on the living cell, our minds should become overwhelmed at the design with an obvious purpose there. When one looks at the diversity and complexity of life, one can immediately ask what caused all of this to be brought into existence. Was it simply chance and undirected natural forces or is there an intelligent designer behind all the complexity we see in nature?

Could natural processes assemble the intricate structures found within living cells? Can chemistry alone account for the origin of life on Earth? What accounts for the origin of the genetic information encoded within living organisms?

Darwin argued that all life was the product of purely undirected forces: Time, chance and natural selection. For example, at the very center of each living cell is a computer called DNA, which determines everything about an organism. Within each cell of man is the entire DNA that determines sex, color of skin, eyes, hair, height and many other inherited characteristics. **(See fig. #64.)**

The human cell is so small, it would take approximately 40,000 of your red blood cells to fill up the letter *o*. The complexity of the cells operating in the human body could be compared to New York City with its millions of citizens, highways, buildings, business and social activities. However, it would be like viewing New York City functioning at full steam in the miniature form of a tiny cell that can only be seen with a high-powered microscope.

Charles Darwin did not know, back in his time, of the existence of the vast intricacies of the cell, not to mention DNA and its genetic code by which all living plant and animal cells in nature function. He thought some chemicals floated in some water, were hit by lightning

Figure 64: The marvelous design of the human cell

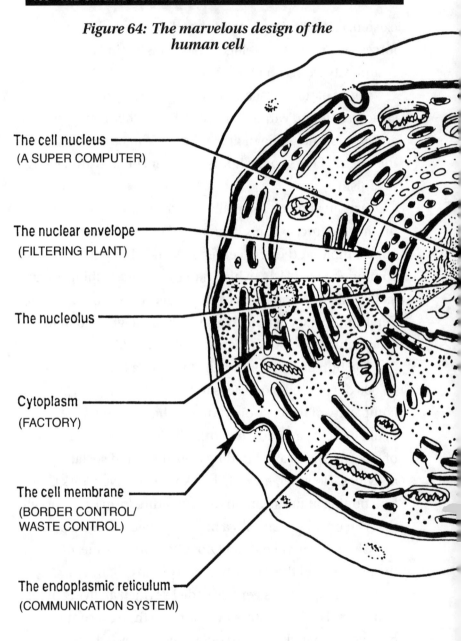

The cell nucleus
(A SUPER COMPUTER)

The nuclear envelope
(FILTERING PLANT)

The nucleolus

Cytoplasm
(FACTORY)

The cell membrane
(BORDER CONTROL/
WASTE CONTROL)

The endoplasmic reticulum
(COMMUNICATION SYSTEM)

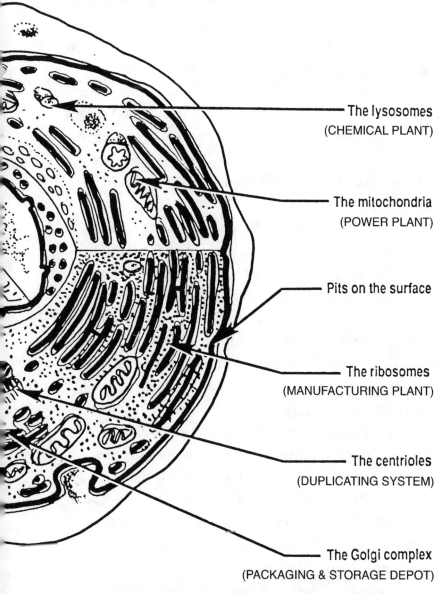

The lysosomes
(CHEMICAL PLANT)

The mitochondria
(POWER PLANT)

Pits on the surface

The ribosomes
(MANUFACTURING PLANT)

The centrioles
(DUPLICATING SYSTEM)

The Golgi complex
(PACKAGING & STORAGE DEPOT)

Within the living cell one sees intelligence of the highest order at work. The more scientists discover about the cell and its intricate and complex construction, the more evident it becomes that a Designer was responsible for our universe.

and — presto — instant life was created as the first cells existed.

Evolutionism is based on the premise that life started with the "simple cell," as Darwin called it. The only problem is there are no "simple cells" with which to start life. All are incredibly brilliant and complex in design and operation. Science has learned so much about the super-tiny, human cell. This knowledge shows the fatal flaw of the entire theory of evolutionism of life proposed by Charles Darwin.

The cell is so brilliantly setup that it takes the top scientists of the world to even begin to understand the complexity of its design. A powerful microscope is needed to see that this incredibly tiny human cell is composed of over three billion parts, each of which are made up of four variants of DNA. The variants are labeled A, T, G or C, which stand for adenine, thymine, guanine and cystosine. These make up the molecules within the cell. The molecules are connected together in an incredible combination of arrangements, creating 80,000 to 100,000 units called genes, which are then combined to form 23 pairs of chromosomes — all within each of the tiny human cells. The genetic material within the cells of all these 100,000 genes is composed collectively of different arrangements of three billion molecules involved in different functions and operations.

It is absolutely obvious there is a colossal Genius behind the design of every cell. The mathematical odds of bringing together three billion different molecules in countless different arrangements for multiple functions in the human body would require trillions upon trillions of years to do so by "random chance." This is why time is the lifeblood of evolutionism.

The estimated 10 trillion cells in the human body function in countless brilliant operations, working together in a coordinated, dazzling, ingeniously engineered design. Can you imagine just how many trillions times trillions of years would be required for 10 trillion cells to learn to work together "by chance" and then continue to faithfully reproduce themselves generation after generation?

The mathematical calculation and scientific odds for evolutionism to randomly reproduce even one, single human cell is infinity times infinity. In other words, it is scientifically impossible for so many factors to come together by random chance and end up creating what Darwin labeled the "simple cell"! To create 10 trillion cells for different functions and designs that would all work together to create a human body by evolutionism's miracle mechanism of random chance is, to put it mildly, utterly absurd.

The living cell represents far more than just random forces; one sees intelligence of the highest order at work. The more scientists discover about the intricate and complex construction of even a single cell, the more evident it becomes that an intelligent Designer had to

Figure 65: Thimbleful of cultured liquid

Powerful technology reveals elaborate microscopic worlds. Worlds so small that a thimble-full of cultured liquid can contain more than four billion single-celled bacteria.

have fashioned our universe. Simple logic points to an intelligent Creator.

Looking at a single-celled animal, a creature so small it takes a high-powered microscope to see it clearly, we find within it an enormous amount of intelligent information.

A Biological Wonder

In the last 50 years, man's understanding of the cell has exploded. Powerful technology reveals elaborate microscopic worlds. Worlds so small that a thimble-full of cultured liquid **(see fig. #65)** can contain more than four billion single-celled bacteria **(see fig. #66)** each packed with circuits, assembly instructions and miniature machines, the complexity of which staggers the mind.

There are molecular machines at the basis of life controlling functions in each simple living cell. Molecular machines, like transportation trucks, carry supplies from one end of the cell to the other. These "machines" capture sunlight and turn it into usable energy. Molecular machinery including the five senses, healing, respiratory action, immune responses, each of which require a host of machines to operate. Where do the machines come

Figure 66: Four billion single-celled bacteria

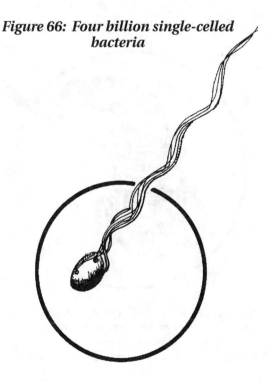

from, how did their parts arrive and how were they assembled? Evolutionism doesn't have a clue. We are led to believe that unintelligent forces somehow produced the most amazing molecular engineering feat known to mankind and told these are mere coincidences.

Consider the One-Cell Bacterial Flagellum

The bacterial germ may be thought of as a simple organism, but it actually reveals amazingly complex engineering. The bacterial flagellum **(see fig. #67)** with all of its parts — propeller, hookerage, drive shaft and motor, functions as a molecular motor that propels some of the

Figure 67: Bacterial flagellum

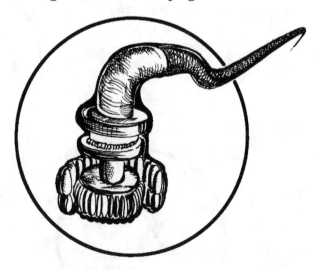

The bacterial flagellum with all of its parts — propeller, hookerage, drive shaft and motor, functions as a molecular motor that propels some of the tiny, microscopic, one-celled bacterial creatures through liquid. It is impossible to consider this as a "chance-assembly" of parts.

tiny, microscopic, one-celled bacterial creatures through liquid. It depends on a system of intricately arranged mechanical parts. When parts of these tiny bacterial creatures are magnified 50,000 times, one discovers a marvel of engineering brilliance on a miniaturized scale. It is impossible to consider this as a "chance-assembly" of parts.

Speaking of miniaturization, the flagellum motor weighs almost nothing, whereas the smallest man-made electric motor weighs .37 grams and is about the size of a housefly, one millionth of an inch in diameter. Eight million of these flagellum motors can fit in the cross-section of a human hair. There are no known motors of any kind that are as rapid, efficient and as small as the flagellum motor. The motorized propeller tail enables them to swim, powered along by a flow of protons much like a man-made electric motor is empowered by a flow of electrons.

The motor of these tiny machines can run at 100,000 revolutions per minute (rpm), propelling itself through water in a manner equivalent to an adult human swimming at 60 mph. **(See fig. #68.)** Even though spinning that fast, they can stop on a dime, turn and shift directions, spinning 100,000 rpm in the other direction. Just like on an outboard motor of a motorboat, a large number of parts are essential to proper functioning.

The flagellar motor has two gears, forward and backward, is water-cooled, uses proton motion force,

Figure 68: 60 mph adult swimmer

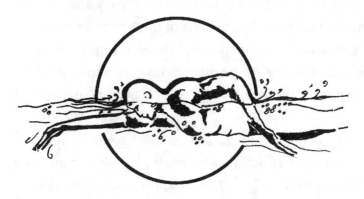

The flagellum motor can run at 100,000 revolutions per minute (rpm), propelling itself through water in a manner equivalent to an adult human swimming at 60 mph.

has a drive shaft, stator (studs/C ring), hook (Universal joint), rotor (S ring and M ring), filament (propeller) and bushing (L ring and P ring). **(See fig. #69.)** How could this motor have developed through the blind chance of natural selection?

Remember the mousetrap with its five basic components. If any one of these five parts is missing or defective, the mechanism will not work. All parts must be present simultaneously for the trap to function properly. This applies to living biological machines, such as the bacterial flagellum. The flagellum (a lash-like appendage that "motors" the movement of the cell) is composed of about 40 protein parts, which are necessary for it to work as a machine. If any of the parts are missing, it won't work or even have the capacity to be assembled.

How could a living machine like this be constructed gradually? Without all the parts in place there would be no value to the rest of the organism. As well, there is nothing within the laws of nature to preserve the construction of such a biological machine until all the parts can evolve to the point the machine will properly function. There

Figure 69: Bacterial flagellum

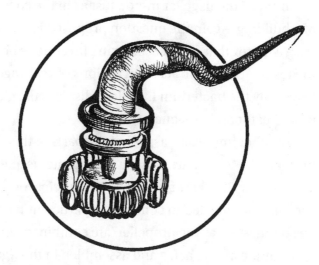

Obviously the bacterium flagellum displays the glory of a wise Creator and Designer.

must be an intelligent designer and builder behind such a biological machine as a flagellum.

Not only must all the pieces be in place, what is more significantly complex is the process and precise sequence of assembling the parts. Building a living, molecular machine can be compared to the construction of a house. First there is a detailed blueprint for the construction. A foundation must be laid before walls are erected. Plumbing and electrical fixtures are installed before the walls are enclosed. Windows are hung before siding is applied. Shingles come after the plywood sheets are nailed to the rafters. So it is with the construction of a flagellar motor. There is a precise sequence in the assembly of the flagellar motor, just as in the construction of a building. Again the question proposed is, "Could such a motor that far exceeds man's inventions be the result of a cosmic accident billions of years ago?" Obviously the bacterium flagellum displays the glory of a wise Creator and Designer.

Another important aspect of the parts of this flagellar motor is that each part is made up of proteins and amino acids. Of the 30,000 various types of proteins, only the specific ones needed to construct a particular part of the flagellum, such as the propeller, are combined with the appropriate amino acids and assembled in the right order and placement for the flagellum to work. Much like letters of the alphabet, if properly arranged, will construct an understandable sentence, amino acids must be properly assembled to form the correct protein. If letters are simply selected at random with no order, there will be no sense. So it is with proteins, each type must be assembled in the right sequence or the motor will not allow the part to fit or function in the overall plan and purpose of the motor.

Instead the part will become useless and render the entire machine inoperable, possibly destroying the machine. The result could be similar to the manner in which a mother's body may reject a fetus if there is something drastically wrong with the overall development of the fetus.

As we consider this information, it is obvious that there is a guiding hand in the making of each part and the assembling of the parts in their proper order. The instructions for the living organism to make and assemble the parts are found in the DNA of the tiny, one-celled creature. The magnitude of difficulty that chance could form the instructions within the DNA of the most simple, one-celled creature is inconceivable.

Think of what the chances of forming two lines of Shakespeare by merely dropping the squares of letters from a *Scrabble* game onto a table are.

"To be or not to be

That's the question."

Yet the genetic instructions to build proteins of the most simple, one-celled creature would require hundreds of pages of printed text.

The DNA instructions for a human being would require three billion individual characters. Bill Gates (of *Microsoft*) has stated that he has never come close to producing a software program with instructions like that found in DNA.

What is your final answer? 1. God. 2. God. 3. God. 4.

God. The answer is quite obvious. Only the fool responds.

> The fool says in his heart, "There is no God." (Psa. 53:1).

The Boob Tube

A living creature is, in one way, like a television set. The laws of physics and chemistry that operate the set cannot explain its origin. No matter how much time and chance are involved, television sets simply are not the product of the laws of nature. The design of a television set reveals a creative act, with just the right materials, for a specific purpose; the observer immediately recognizes a television set could not develop on its own.

Can Aluminum Fly?

Will mixing aluminum with rubber and gasoline make it fly? Not unless intelligence is used to arrange all the ingredients in just the right way to make an airplane. And what makes an airplane fly? The wings? The engine? The pilot? None of these in themselves can make an airplane fly. In fact, an airplane is a collection of parts that, in and of themselves, are incapable of flight. Its ability to fly cannot be derived from the properties of aluminum, rubber and gasoline. Its ability to fly is really the result of the total organization of all the parts by an intelligent designer and builder.

So it is with a living system. Each living cell is a coordinated set of non-living molecules. Its ability to grow, react and reproduce does not come from the *properties* of the molecules involved, but from the intelligent *organization* of them — the result of an intelligent creation. And the kind of arrangement observed is not the same as is seen in snowflakes or pebbles in a creek bed. It's a special type of organization found only in those objects that are the products of a deliberate and intelligent creation.

The orderly and understandable ways in which living systems operate reflect God's faithful care of His creation. Each system originated in the mind of God — not in the properties of matter.

If the evidence is so clear, why don't more see it? Paul answers this in Romans 1:18; in an effort to validate their disbelief in God, people suppress the truth. The problem is not with the mind; it's a heart problem.

The Human Brain

There is one particular aspect of design so powerful and convincing, to attempt to come up with an evolutionary explanation for its origins boggles the mind. I am referring to the human brain — the greatest concentration of chemo-neurological order and complexity in the entire known physical universe. The brain is a video camera, a library, a computer and a communications center — all in one. And the more the brain is used, the finer it becomes! Remarkable purpose and interdependence is observed within the brain. Every part works for the benefit of the entire body. The adult brain weighs about three pounds, yet it handles the information of 1,000 supercomputers.[19] The fundamental unit within the brain is the neuron, or nerve cell; each brain contains about 10 billion of these neurons. **(See fig. #70.)**

During the first nine months of a human fetus' life, neurons form at the astounding rate of 25,000 per minute. Eventually, each neuron is in contact with about 10,000 other neurons, making the total number of connections about 100 trillion — a number equivalent to all the leaves

Figure 70: The incredible human brain

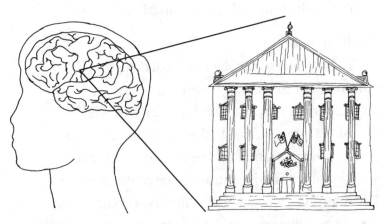

The human brain is the most complex system in the entire universe. It handles the information equal to 1,000 supercomputers— enough to fill all the major libraries in the world.

on all the trees of an imaginary forest the size of the U.S. Thus, the brain holds enough information to fill all the major libraries in the world.

At any given moment, approximately 10 percent of the brain cells are working — at a speed far superior to the fastest computers. And even today's supercomputers have a storage capacity 1,000 times less than that of the human brain. The potential brain capacity is estimated as at least equivalent to that of 25 million volumes, or a 500-mile-long bookshelf! This is far larger than the 20 million volumes housed in the Library of Congress. Clearly, the brain is far more advanced than any computer ever produced.

One ongoing area of brain research involves the separate functions of the left and right hemispheres. The left side of the body is mainly controlled by the right side of the brain and the right side of the body is controlled by the left side of the brain. The brain's functioning capacity in the areas of language and analytical problem-solving are found in the left hemisphere; the right hemisphere, in contrast, controls visual and artistic ideas.

Perhaps the absurd, and conflicting, evolutionary ideas about the evolving of the brain are a result of an imbalance between the two sides of the atheistic brain. Evolutionary thinking appears to be the result of right hemisphere activity — very creative; but there is a lack of the use of the left side of the brain where logical reasoning occurs! The brain truly provides an ultimate design challenge for evolutionists.

It seems strange that the well-known evolutionist, the late Carl Sagan, said in one breath that if we could receive one line of information from outer space, it would lead to the salvation of man. Yet, in the next breath, he stated that a single cell, coded with enough information to fill a volume the size of an encyclopedia, could arise by chance with no intelligence sponsoring it. Only a fool could make such a statement. "The fool says in his heart, 'There is no God'" (Psa. 14:1).

Design or Chance?

Dr. Wernher von Braun was a leading scientist in the U.S. space program until his death in the late 1970s. His remarks, from an article in *Applied Christianity* about the design of the universe, were published in the May 1974 *Bible Science Newsletter*. He said in part,

> One cannot be exposed to the law and order of the universe without concluding that there must be design and purpose behind it all. ... The better we understand the intricacies of the universe and all it harbors, the more reason we have found to marvel at the inherent design upon which it is based. To be forced to believe only one conclusion — that everything in the universe happened by chance — would violate the very objectivity of science itself. What random process could produce the brains of a man or the system of the human eye? They (evolutionists) challenge science to prove the existence of God. But must we really light a candle

to see the sun? They say they cannot visualize a Designer. Well, can a physicist visualize an electron? What strange rationale makes some physicists accept the inconceivable electron as real, while refusing to accept the reality of a Designer on the grounds that they cannot conceive Him? It is in scientific honesty that I endorse the presentation of alternative theories for the origin of the universe, life and man in the science classroom. It would be an error to overlook the possibility that the universe was planned rather than happening by chance.

Have you not known? Have you not heard? The everlasting God, the LORD, the Creator of the ends of the earth, neither faints nor is weary. His understanding is unsearchable (Isa. 40:28).

CHAPTER FOURTEEN

The Evolving Oscillating Gold Quartz Watch

It is pleasant to listen to wise words, but a fool's speech brings him to ruin. Since he begins with a foolish premise, his conclusion is sheer madness (Eccl. 10:12, 13 LB).

Figure 71: The iron atom

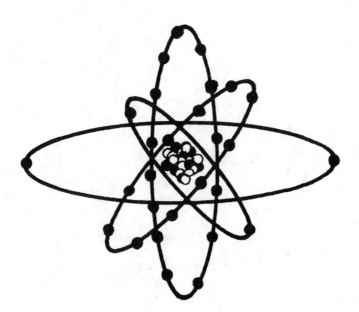

Figure 72: Lump of iron ore

Picture one tiny atom of iron resting deep within the core of the Earth. This tiny atom is so small it would take literally millions of them to cover the head of a pin. As time passes, the currents of molten lava cause other tiny atoms of iron to pass near this iron atom, and somehow they become attracted to one another. **(See fig. #71.)**

As tens of thousands of years pass, more and more iron atoms are similarly captured. Million of years pass and the once invisible iron atom now becomes a tiny visible speck of iron about the size of a grain of sand. Additional hundreds of millions of years pass, and the speck of iron continues to grow to a lump of iron ore about the size of a silver dollar. As the intense heat and pressure increase inside the Earth's center, the lump of iron becomes a purified piece of refined steel. **(See fig. #72.)**

One day, from the mouth of an erupting volcano, the molten lump of refined steel is hurled skyward. While falling to the Earth, the steel separates into droplets that come to rest within inches of each other on the surface of the planet. These tiny droplets of steel cool and solidify. **(See fig. #73.)**

As many thousands of years pass, the elements of nature grind away at the tiny pieces of steel. Wind, rain, lightning wear on them, and the pieces begin to assume crude forms. Shapes — squares, circles, rectangles — begin to appear.

More millennia pass, and the elements continue to shape the metal pieces into more unusual and refined forms, such as gears, pins, sprockets, springs and tiny levers. **(See fig. #74.)**

Suddenly, one day without any warning, an earthquake violently shakes the tiny pieces of steel — and by a freak act of nature, all the pieces are thrown together in just the right way so that, lo and behold, a crude pocket watch has come into being.

As more time passes, gradually the watch chain is transformed into a lovely gold wristband. Still later, the main spring is replaced by an oscillating piece of refined quartz. Time continues to shrink the entire mechanism so that one particular part takes on the form and nature of a battery, which becomes energized by another freak act of nature. After being submerged — having been knocked accidentally into a river by a passing avalanche of dirt,

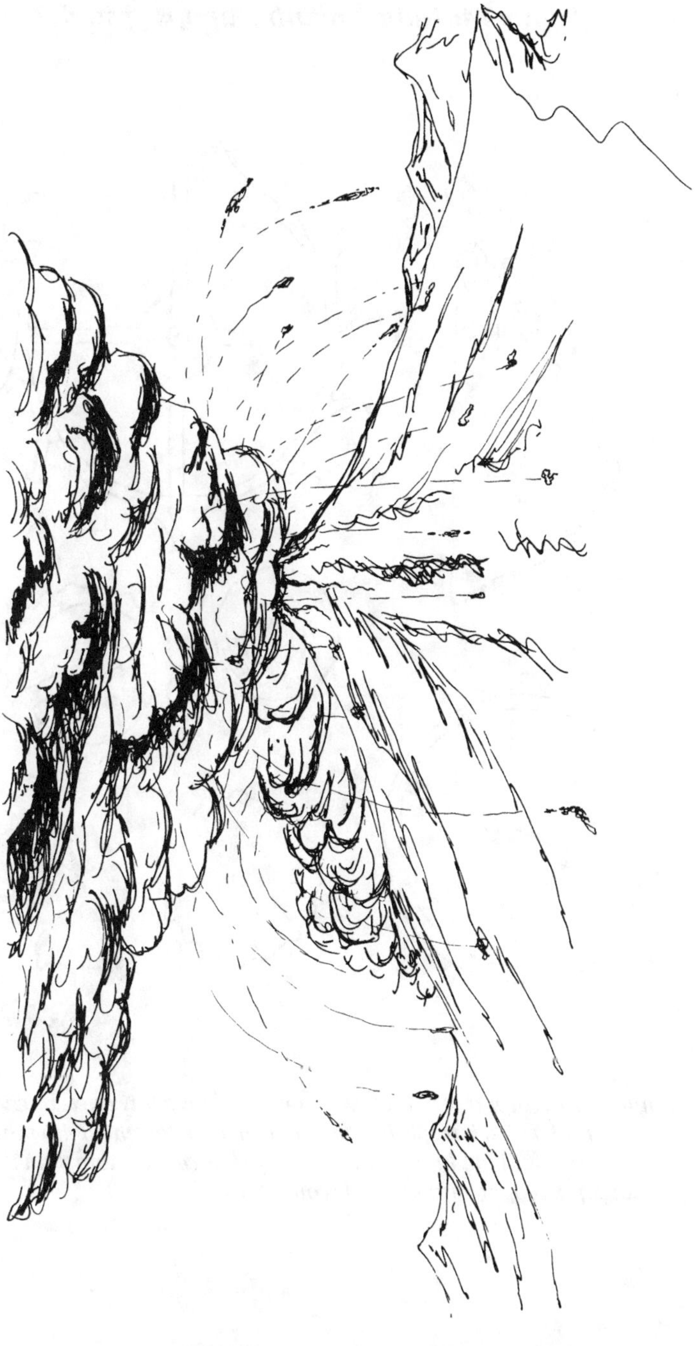

Figure 73: "Nature" at work

Figure 74: Nature refining lumps of steel???

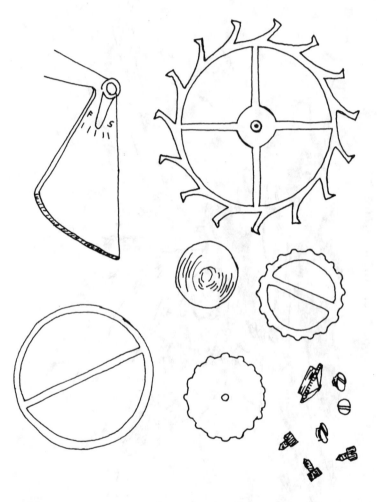

Could nature, over a period of years, produce these tiny parts by chance? Each part of a watch is specifically made to work together with other parts. They could not have come about by chance any more than the complex parts of the human body could have.

mud and gravel — it receives a low voltage charge of electrical current from a passing electrical eel. Oh yes, the entire mechanism has become sealed and waterproofed to a depth of 100 meters.

Thus, after millions of years, the crude lump of iron has evolved into an efficient and accurate timepiece — one that is shockproof, waterproof and dustproof. This precision mechanism came about, not as a result of any intelligence, but by unintelligible, blind chance. **(See fig. # 75.)**

Millions of years pass and man emerges on the scene. In time, he becomes civilized. One day while out for a stroll, a civilized man happens to come across a dry creek bed and the unusual mechanism. Not knowing what it is, he takes it home with him.

After some time, he notices the numbers on its face correspond with the passing of time. He also discovers it fits nicely on his wrist. Since finding the first watch, our civilized man has returned to the area of the original discovery where several additional watches, each slightly different, are found.

After several months, his collection of watches is growing. It's not long before the idea enters his mind that he might be able to sell or trade these objects to others, so he opens up a business. Nature has truly blessed his life. What a stroke of luck to find such a useful object which nature has evolved through time!

Is this the most ridiculous story ever concocted?

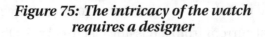

*Figure 75: The intricacy of the watch
requires a designer*

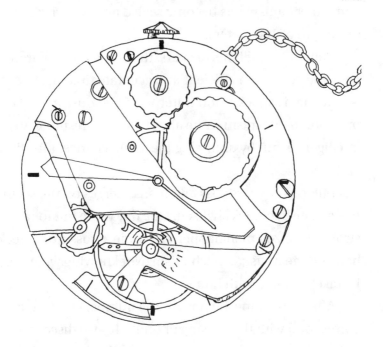

Not by a long shot. Evolutionists relentlessly attempt to convince the public that man — incredibly more complex than the watch — has arrived through just such a process. How absurd!

The evolutionism/creation science debate boils down to this: chance versus design. The human race either originated by design or strictly by chance; no more, no less. Chance assumes no Supreme Being; design requires one.

If we are here by design, then God must be the

Designer. Where did He come from? The Word does not explain the origin of the Creator — only of the creation. It simply states that God is. One either accepts this declaration in faith or he doesn't. "Preposterous," says the evolutionist, "What kind of science is that?" On the other hand, how brilliant is it to expect intelligent creatures to actually believe that chance alone has produced the complex universe through the evolutionary process. And the evolutionist has absolutely no explanation as to the origin of matter which comprised the first crude form of life — it simply somehow existed.

Two views — each at opposite ends of the spectrum. One declares divine direction. The other assumes blind chance. When we examine the intricate assembly of a watch, we cannot begin to conceive of its creation by chance. When we look at the ever so much more complex nature of the human being, how can we suppose that man originated without the guiding hand of God? Chance is just not good enough.

> How many are your works, O LORD! In wisdom you made them all; the earth is full of your creatures (Psa. 104:24).

CHAPTER FIFTEEN

The "Anthropic Coincidences" (Intelligent Accidents)

A great testimony to God's existence is the reality of the universe with its precision design and beauty.

The heavens declare the glory of God; the skies proclaim the work of his hands (Psa. 19:1).

For since the creation of the world God's invisible qualities — his eternal power and divine nature — have been clearly seen, being understood from what has been made, so that men are without excuse (Rom. 1:20).

Everywhere in creation we see evidence of God's existence and of His greatness and power. All the amazing designs demand we recognize a great Designer Who has tremendous intelligence and knowledge.

The Anthropic Principle

It was common for scientists of the 18th and 19th centuries to argue over whether or not the universe reveals design in its origin. Scientists of the 20th century became "enlightened" and refused to even entertain such "religious notions." Yet if one looks, without preconceptions, at the delicately integrated and coordinated universe, it is only natural to conclude that it was created by a tremendously intelligent and Creative Being. For instance, how can one account for the remarkable complexity of plants and animals, let alone the incredible creature, man, without recognizing the existence of a Designer? Those who refuse to see the obvious do so because of their rebellion toward God.

> They exchanged the truth of God for a lie, and worshiped and served created things rather than the Creator — who is forever praised (Rom. 1:25).

The idea that the universe reveals design was ousted from the science of biology in the last century like prayer was removed from public schools in recent years. However, consideration of design is reappearing in cosmology — a branch of astronomy involving the origin, structure and space-time relationships of the universe. It is now vogue for non-Christian cosmologists and physicists to speak of the "anthropic principle," which demands that life on the Earth is no accident.

For the universe to have "evolved" in such a way that it would support life, a large number of highly improbable coincidences would have had to occur. The anthropic principle studies these coincidences and concludes that there is design in the universe, for without just one of these "coincidences" life on Earth would be impossible.

Consider Gravity

The Earth could not support life unless the universe itself had the right physical properties. The anthropic principle reflects an incredible number of "cosmic coincidences" that make life possible. For example, the initial creation had to have occurred with just the right degree of intensity for our present universe to have been formed. If it had occurred with too little velocity, the universe would have collapsed back in on itself shortly after creation occurred because of gravitational forces. If it had occurred with too much speed, the matter of which it consists would have moved so quickly away that it would have been impossible for galaxies and solar systems to have formed. To state it another way, the force and importance of gravity must be fine-tuned to allow the universe to expand at precisely the right rate, accurate to within one part in 10^{60}. The fact that the force of gravity just happens to be the right number with "such stunning accuracy," writes physicist Paul Davies, " is surely one of the great mysteries of cosmology."[xx] Furthermore, all the planets in our solar system help to maintain equilibrium of the Earth's orbit.

Chance and Scientific Method

If the universe is a product of chance, then the scientific method could never be relied upon; the results of an experiment could vary from time to time. The scientific method depends upon a personal belief or faith in underlying principles for which the evolutionary theory of time + matter + chance does not allow. A very revealing statement regarding the atheist's position in the quest for honestly seeking truth was shared by a well-known evolutionist, Bertrand Russell:

> Though we cannot validate the scientific method, we accept it because it seems to work.

In other words, although the belief that creation is the result of chance violates the scientific method of seeking truth, evolutionists choose to ignore the discrepancy in order that they may remain god of their own lives.

How Random Chance Works

We have previously considered the incredible mathematical odds that life could arise by chance. The principle of calculating such incredible odds can be easily understood in the following illustration.

When flipping a coin, there is one chance in two it will turn up heads. If there were three coins, how likely is it that all three would come up heads (or tails) if they were spilled out on the table? The chances of this happening can be figured by a simple mathematical equation. In this case, it is expressed as one in six, one (chance) x two (sides) x three (coins) = six. **(See fig. #76.)**

Now as one starts adding more coins, the odds quickly increase against the chance of all the coins landing heads up. And if another criterion is added, the number immediately increases by leaps and bounds. For example,

Figure 76: How random chance works

what are the chances of just 10 coins all being blindly arranged perfectly according to their different dates, the earliest first and right on up to the latest? The calculation is figured this way: 1 x 2 x 3 x 4 x 5 x 6 x 7x 8 x 9 x 10 = 3,628,800 or one in 3,628,800 chances. That is with only 10 different coins. Would you bet your life's savings on such a proposition? Not if you are smart.

Living creatures are not composed of only 10 parts, but millions and millions of components — and all must be in the right place and working harmoniously for proper survival. When it comes to the precision of the universe, the odds would be one against a number so large that the number of electrons in the universe would be small in comparison.

If a person had one chance in 10, he might bet on a horse race. One chance in a million is ridiculous, but he might bet in a lottery if it didn't cost him much. One in a billion? Never. One in a trillion? Be serious! But evolutionists not only want us to bet on a number, followed by at least thousands of 500-page volumes full of zeros; they also want us to agree it happened that way because it couldn't have occurred the other way! They want a person to bet his immortal soul on it. Remember poor Buford? **(See fig. #46.)**

The famous physicist, Albert Einstein, has been quoted as saying: "God Almighty does not throw dice." Is it any wonder why mathematicians can have serious doubts about evolutionism?

Noted English astronomer, Sir Fred Hoyle, acknowledged the universe contains so many "anthropic coincidences" (intelligent accidents) that there is no logical escape from the conclusion that some higher "intelligence" was involved. Hoyle's arguments are even more impressive when one considers his admission, "I am not a Christian, nor am I likely to become one as far as I can tell."[xxi]

Life on Earth

Let us examine just 10 of the "anthropic coincidences" (intelligent accidents) of which Sir Fred Hoyle was speaking, in regard to the absolute essentials required for life to exist on planet Earth: Distance for the sun, orbital speed, rotational spin, axis tilt, wobble angle, moon size and distance from the Earth, diameter, oceanic level, crust thickness and atmospheric content. These 10 coincidences represent 10 amazing coins that all come up heads.

1) Distance from the sun

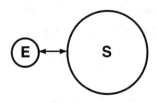

Figure 77

The distance of the Earth from the sun is 93 million miles. The average temperature of the sun's surface is 11,500° F. Sunspots are between one to two million degrees Fahrenheit. Scientists have determined if the temperature were only 50° F. more or less for just one year, life would cease to exist. Fifty degrees is less than ½ of one percent of the average surface temperature of the sun. It appears the temperature of the sun was designed expressly for the purpose of making the Earth hospitable to the existence of life. Coin #1 comes up heads.

2) Orbital speed

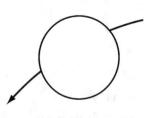

Figure 78

The Earth is moving around the sun at 67,000 miles per hour, or about 18 miles per second. If the Earth were to slow down to six miles per second, life would burn up. If the Earth's speed were increased to 40 miles per second, the planet would be thrown out of its orbit into the coldness of space, and life would come to a quick end. It appears the speed of the Earth around the sun was designed expressly for the purpose of making the Earth hospitable to the existence of life. Coin #2 comes up heads. That's two in a row!

3) Rotational spin

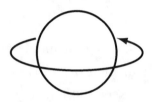

Figure 79

The Earth turns once a day in just the perfect manner so one doesn't burn up in the day or freeze at night. It revolves at a speed of 1,000 miles per hour at the equator. If it rotated slower on its axis, all life would cease to exist, either by freezing cold at night or by burning heat during the day.

If, for instance, the Earth rotated at 100 miles per hour (Mercury's rotation requires 59 days to complete, while the rotation of Venus requires 243 days), the days and nights would be 10 times as long. The heat would build up in the summer months to the point that life could not exist. The temperature during the winter months would drop to as much as -240° F. and life could no longer exist.

Actually, if the yearly average temperature on Earth rose or fell only a few degrees, most life would either quickly roast or freeze. The change would upset the water-ice relationship and other balances, with disastrous results. Or can you imagine the Earth's rotation requiring 10 hours? Such is the case with Jupiter and Saturn, rather than Earth's 24-hour rotation. Man's normal 16 hours of being awake would be interrupted with a constant adjustment: Ten hours of daylight and six hours of darkness — and then the reverse — six hours of daylight and 10 hours of darkness. It appears the rotational speed of the Earth was designed expressly for the purpose of making the Earth hospitable to the existence of life. Coin #3 comes up heads!

4) Axis tilt

Figure 80

The Earth is slightly tilted on its axis at an angle of 23°. The tilt helps to keep the sun's rays in balance so the temperature does not become too hot or too cold for life to exist. If the Earth were tilted at 80° in reference to the sun (as is Uranus), we would not have the four seasons. Without seasons, life would soon disappear. The poles would lie in eternal twilight, and water vapor from the oceans would be carried away by the winds towards both the north and the south, and would freeze when close enough to the poles. In time, huge continents of snow and ice would pile up in the polar regions, leaving most of the Earth a dry desert. Eventually the oceans would disappear completely and rainfall would cease. The accumulated weight of ice at the poles would cause the equator to bulge and, as a result, the rotation of the Earth would drastically change, causing further negative affects for life on the Earth. Other planets' tilts vary significantly: Pluto, 60°; Jupiter and Venus, 3°; Mercury — no tilt at all.

It appears the tilt of the Earth was designed expressly for purpose of making the Earth hospitable for the existence of life. Coin #4 comes up heads. What a coincidence!

5) Wobble angle

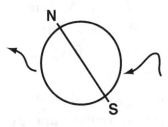

The Earth has a slight wobble of 3°. This helps to deflect the intensity of the sun's rays. If it wobbled more than 3° up, the poles would freeze over, resulting in the shrinking of the oceans,

Figure 81

which in turn would cause more land to exist, eventuating the land to become desert. If it wobbled more than 3° down, the polar caps would melt, causing the oceans to rise; this would in turn cause an absorption of carbon dioxide from the atmosphere which would then limit plant growth — the major producer of oxygen.

It appears the wobble of the Earth was designed expressly for the purpose of making the Earth hospitable for the existence of life. Coin #5 comes up heads. Wow, five in a row!

6) Moon's size and distance from the Earth

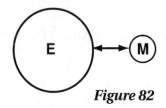

The moon is just the right size and distance from Earth. If it were larger or closer,

Figure 82

oceans would flood much of the low-lying coastal areas. If it were 50,000 miles from the Earth instead of 240,000 miles, the tides along the Texas coastline would break on the Rocky Mountains, producing hurricane winds. The huge swells would overflow onto the lowlands and erode the mountains. And with the continents leveled, it is estimated water would cover the entire surface of the Earth to a depth of a mile and a half. If the moon were smaller or farther out, the tides would be too small to keep our harbors clean and replenished with oxygen, which is essential for the food chain.

It appears both the size and the distance of the moon from the Earth were designed expressly for the purpose of making the Earth hospitable for the existence of life. Coin #6 comes up heads. Wow, six coins — all heads. That's too much!

7) Diameter of the Earth

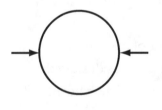

Figure 83

The diameter of the Earth is 8,000 miles. Scientists tell us if the Earth were 1,000 miles more in its diameter, the force of gravity on the Earth would increase, causing a series of chain reactions to occur. The weight of the air would increase, resulting in an increased volume of water on the surface of the Earth, raising the level of the oceans and causing great areas of the Earth to be flooded.

If the Earth were 1,000 miles less in diameter, the force of gravity would decrease, allowing the atmosphere to escape into space. Not only would life be impossible, meteorites would constantly pound the surface of the Earth causing it to become like the surface of the moon — a frozen, dead planet.

It appears the diameter of the Earth was designed expressly for the purpose of making the Earth hospitable for the existence of life. Coin #7 comes up heads. Hmm, something seems fishy here.

8) Ocean level

Figure 84

Chapter four examined the peculiar attributes of water, one of the most complex and unique substances known to man. The characteristics of water differ from almost all the rules common to other chemicals. Water is totally out of step with the properties of the other elements. It seems it has been designed expressly for the purpose of making the Earth hospitable for the existence of life.

The Earth is the only planet with huge bodies of water; 70 percent of its surface area is covered with water. A few planets have moisture floating as vapor on their surface, but not large bodies of liquid water as on Earth. The Earth's oceans act as a thermostat, maintaining temperature stability. Water is unique; it absorbs large amounts of heat without much alteration in its temperature. If it were not for the tremendous amount of water on the Earth, there would be far greater day and night temperature variations. If the ocean level were lower, we would have hotter and longer summers. Many parts of the surface would be hot enough to boil water in the day, yet cold enough to freeze water at night. If the ocean levels were greater, carbon dioxide would be absorbed from the air, snuffing out plant life — the largest producer of oxygen.

It seems the level of the oceans has been designed expressly for the purpose of making the Earth hospitable for the existence of life. Coin #8 comes up heads. Wait a minute; I think this has been rigged!

9) Crust's thickness

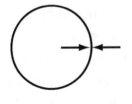

Figure 85

The thickness of the Earth's crust is just right. Scientists have determined that if approximately 10 feet of solid matter were added to the Earth's entire surface, the oxygen in the atmosphere would become oxidized (removed). Considering the diameter of the Earth is 8,000 miles, the fact that 10 feet would make such a difference causes one to have reservations that the Earth's thickness happened by chance.

It appears the thickness of the Earth's crust was designed expressly for the purpose of making the Earth hospitable for the existence of life. Coin #9 comes up heads. I'm becoming very suspicious now. No one can flip nine coins in a row — and all of them come up heads.

Figure 86

10) Atmospheric content

What keeps the constancy of the Earth's atmosphere? Mars and Venus are about 90 percent carbon dioxide, whereas the Earth is 21 percent oxygen, 75 percent nitrogen and almost no carbon dioxide. What maintains this constancy of the Earth's atmosphere in a manner that happens to be essential for life?

One scientist contended that for the atmosphere to remain constant is a miracle — like riding a bicycle blindfolded during rush hour and not getting hurt.

Consider the oxygen level: It is 21 percent. If it were 25 percent, it would be impossible to grow forests because of fires, which would be ignited by lightning during electrical storms. Even pouring rain couldn't put out the fires. If the oxygen level were only 19 percent, just two percent less, we'd suffocate. If it were 10 percent more, the Earth would explode like a huge ball of fire.

It appears the oxygen level in the Earth's atmosphere was designed expressly for the purpose of making the Earth hospitable for the existence of life. Coin #10 comes up heads. What a coincidence! I'm no sucker; I've been tricked!

More Coincidences

Plants are chemical factories that pick up carbon dioxide — the waste product that both man and animals exhale. **(See fig. #87.)** Plants convert this carbon dioxide into oxygen, which both man and animals require for survival. Suppose plants needed the same element, oxygen, as man needs. They would be competitors, and living creatures would be in jeopardy.

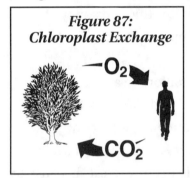

Figure 87:
Chloroplast Exchange

It appears the exchange in gases between plant and animal kingdoms was designed expressly for the purpose of making the Earth hospitable for the existence of life. **(See fig. #88.)**

And the coins just keep coming up heads. What a coincidence! Either two-headed coins are being used or else someone has deliberately directed the outcome. Someone has:

> Who hath measured the waters in the hollow of his hand, and meted out heaven with the span, and comprehended the dust of the earth in a measure, and weighed the mountains in scales, and the hills in a balance? (Isa. 40:12 KJV).

Newton's Model

Sir Isaac Newton (1642-1727) was a British scientist,

Figure 88: The interdependence of plants and animals

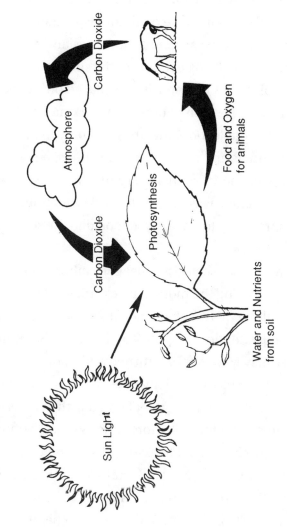

Plants are chemical factories which pick up carbon dioxide a waste product of both man and animal. Plants convert carbon dioxide into oxygen, which both man and animals require to survive. If plants needed oxygen, all life would be in jeopardy. It appears that plants were designed expressly for the purpose of making earth hospitable for life.

mathematician and philosopher who formulated and proved the law of gravity. That a maker is required for anything produced is a lesson Sir Isaac Newton was able to forcefully teach to one of his atheist-scientist friends. Sir Isaac had an accomplished artesian design and construct a small-scale model of the solar system. When the project was finished, it wa s placed on a large table in a room in Newton's home. The workman had done a commendable job, simulating not only the various sizes of the planets and their relative positions, but also constructing the model so that everything rotated and orbited when a crank was turned. It was fascinating to watch — particularly for anyone schooled in the sciences. **(See fig. #89.)**

Newton's atheist-scientist colleague came by for a visit. After examining the model, he remarked, "My, what an exquisite thing this is? Who made it?" Newton, as if he weren't paying attention, responded, "Nobody." Stopping his inspection, Newton's friend turned and said, "Sir Isaac, evidently you misunderstood my question. I asked who made this model?" Newton was delighted with his friend's reaction, and replied in a still more serious tone, "Nobody. That you see just happened to assume the form it now has." Still not discerning Newton's crafty intentions, the atheist abruptly responded with, "Sir Isaac, you must think I'm gullible to believe that. Of course somebody made it."

Newton then spoke to his friend in a polite but

Figure 89: Newton's model of the solar system

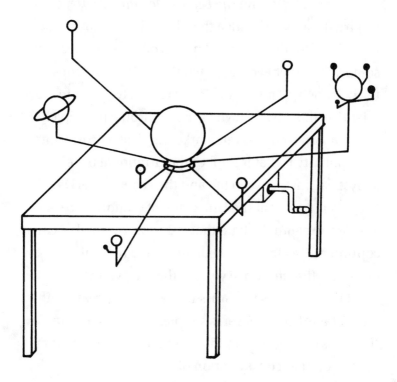

firm way. "This thing is but a puny imitation of a much grander system whose laws you know, and I am not able to convince you this mere toy is without a designer and maker; yet you profess to believe the great original, from which this design is taken, has come into being without either designer or maker. Now tell me, by what sort of reasoning do you reach such an unreasonable conclusion?"

A Fightin' Word for Physicists: Anthropic

A recent article in *The Dallas Morning News*[xxii] by Tom Siegfried states, "The idea that the universe was meant for life refuses to die." Siegfried points out that for decades, some scientists have suggested that certain features of the cosmos are "just right" for life to evolve. "But to many scientists the idea, known as the anthropic principle, is about as popular as telemarketing. The reason for its unpopularity is that it implies the "irrational belief in a mystical link between life and the cosmos." As David Gross, a physicist at the University of California, Santa Barbara, exclaims, "I hate the anthropic principle." Gross continues, "My feeling is that anthropic reasoning is kind of a virus. It seems once you get the bug, you can't get rid of it." Why does Dr. Gross find anthropic reasoning unpalatable? The answer is simple. Dr. Gross responds, "It smells of religion and intelligent design."[xxiii] In other words, it forces consideration of God.

How long will you say such things? Your words are a blustering wind (Job 8:2).

CHAPTER SIXTEEN

The Earth Was Made For Habitation

Figure 90: "The earth was made for habitation"

The entire theory of life arising spontaneously at the direction of blind chance is totally absurd, and only a fool would embrace such a concept. God's entire creation was designed with a purpose in mind.

> … He did not create it to be empty, but formed it to be inhabited … (Isa. 45:18).

In Genesis 1:11, the Bible reveals how God filled the Earth with living things, and fashioned it as a beautiful home for mankind.

The Theory of Quantum Physics Reinforces Biblical Creation

In spite of man's attempts to rid himself of any concept of a Creator, the science of quantum physics seems to confirm the reality of there being a purpose in creation. **(See fig. #90.)**

Quantum physics is a scientific theory pertaining to energy; it suggests man may really be the focus of creation, as even this excerpt, from an atheistic, evolutionary magazine (*Science Digest),* reports:

> Is the earth the center of the universe? The question seems preposterous in these enlightened times, but for millennia the answer was an obvious yes. A few Greek philosophers argued that the earth revolved around the sun, but any fool could look up in the sky and see they were wrong. And though centuries of scientific thought have given proof to the contrary, now, despite all this, some philosophically minded physicists and others are pushing the notion that we are indeed the most important planet in the cosmos. In a sense, they argue, the creationists are right, and man is in the middle — not because God says so, but because the apparently ironclad laws of quantum mechanics say so.[xxiv]

Isaiah 45:18 reveals God made the Earth to be inhabited. Is there life outside the Earth? We do not know; as yet there is no evidence of such; still, it is not impossible. We do know the Earth is remarkably and exquisitely made for life. Life hangs on a delicate balance which only God could have designed and sustained. The Earth may not be the center of the physical universe, but it is the central battleground for mankind. Man is certainly far more than just a piece of dirt!

Order of Creation of the Earth, Sun, Moon & Stars

The Bible declares the Earth was created before the sun, moon and stars. God first created the building blocks for His creation: Space, matter and energy. Then He separated day from night. On the second day of creation He made the "expanse," separating the water on the Earth from the water above the Earth. On the third day He made the dry ground appear and put vegetation on the Earth. Until the third day, His attention seemed totally focused upon the Earth. **(See fig. #91.)**

See what happened on the fourth day:

> God made two great lights — the greater light to govern the day and the lesser light to govern the night. He also made the stars. God set them in the expanse of the sky to give light on the earth, to govern the day and the night, and to separate light from darkness. And God saw that it was good. And there was evening, and there was morning — the fourth day (Gen. 1:16-19).

Some have been troubled by the biblical account of the order of creation. They wonder how God could have made day and night on the first day when He did not create the sun or the moon until the fourth day. And how

Figure 91: The days of creation

Day One:
And God said, "Let there be light" … God called the light "day" and the darkness he called "night."

Day Two:
And God said, "Let there be an expanse between the waters to separate water from water" … God called the expanse "sky."

Day Three:
And God said, "Let … dry ground appear… Let the land produce vegetation. …"

Day Four:
And God said, "Let there be lights in the expanse of the sky to separate the day from the night, and … as signs to mark seasons and days and years. …."

Day Five:
And God said, "Let the water teem with living creatures, and let birds fly above the earth. …"

Day Six:
And God said, "Let the land produce living creatures according to their kinds. …" Then God said, "Let us make man in our image. …"

(From Gen. 1:3-26 NIV)

was there light without the sun?

Gap Theory Seeks to Provide a Compromise

Proponents of the "Gap Theory"[3] suggest the sun, moon and stars were actually created earlier, but only became visible on the fourth "day." However, the entire theory is built on unstable sand. It proposes there is a gap of millions of years between Genesis 1:1 and Genesis 1:2 during which another creation existed, sinned and was destroyed by judgment. **(See fig. #92.)** Though Scripture never mentions such a creation, many Christians have accepted this theory because it provides a possible compromise for the evolutionists' supposed proof the Earth is billions of years old. However, there is no compelling evidence for the idea the Earth is billions of years old. To the contrary, the bulk of evidence indicates a young Earth, less than 10,000 years old.[4] This supports the conclusions made from a literal reading of Scripture: The Earth is about 6,000 years old. The best argument for the actual creation of the sun, moon and stars on the fourth day is that "...God said ... And it was so" (Gen. 1:14, 15). This is the same formula God used in all of His creative acts. If we accept one verse literally, we must accept all. We either believe God's Word is true, or we don't.

God Doesn't Need a Watch

God is the Creator of the heavens and the Earth.

3 The Gap theory concept is covered in Volume 7 of the Creation Science series
4 The young earth concept is covered in volumes 8 and 9 of the Creation Science Series

Figure 92: Gap therory

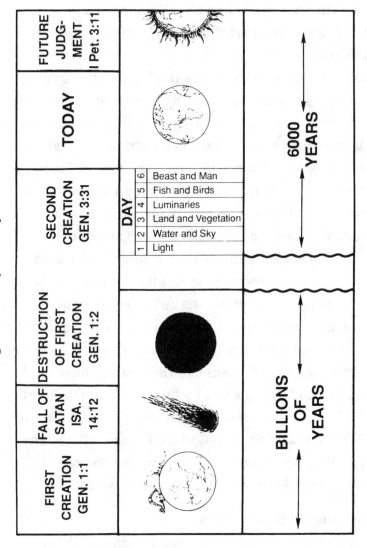

Though He did not create the sun, moon and stars until the fourth day of creation week, He certainly would have no problem keeping track of time. Just because there was, as yet, no sun does not mean God could not have calculated the first three days in time and reported it to us accurately in Scripture. Time is apparently a function of matter: "In the beginning (of time), God created the heavens and the earth (matter)" (Gen. 1:1).

Even man has been able to measure day and night without the usual references of sun and moon. Submarines, today, stay deep in the oceans, often cruising under thick polar ice caps, yet they can accurately measure the passing of days. Astronauts have stayed up in space for months, and using modern technology, keep track of time. Men who have been trapped underground in mine cave-ins or lost in underground caves have managed to maintain a calendar of sorts. One student associated with the University of Texas experimented by living in a cave for six months with no outside contact. Records were kept on a computer. He found he had a consistent internal clock telling him when to get up and when to go to sleep. Nature is full of plants, insects, animals and birds that have accurate internal clocks. Certainly the all-wise God can gauge time without the use of the sun or moon.

Plants Were Created Before the Sun

If a day in Genesis chapter one were millions of years

long, plants would never have made it until the creation
of the sun. But it would have been very easy for them to
exist for just one day in total darkness. This is another
testimony in favor of a literal 24-hour day.

God: The Source of Light

Since God is the source of light, He certainly does
not need the sun and other stars in order to have light.
Besides, even man can make light without stars.

The Book of Revelation tells us the inhabitants of the
new Earth " … will not need the light of a lamp or the
light of the sun, for the Lord God will give them light. …"
(Rev. 22:5). Also, the tree of life will be "… yielding its fruit
every month …" (Rev. 22:2). To us it seems inconceivable
there could be "months" without a sun. However, this
is certainly no problem for Almighty God. Before the
sun was created, the light no doubt stemmed from God
Himself — the perfect light.[5]

A Matter of Faith

What one believes about the first six days of creation
is based largely upon one's ideas about the source of the
universe and upon circumstantial, scientific evidence.

In other words, it is a matter of faith; not blind faith, but
circumstantial faith — faith based on reason, logic and

5   Scientifically, there is always light — measurable electromagnetic radiation
(light wave) — wherever there is any matter at all at a temperature above
absolute zero, but such radiation is usually not visible unless the matter is at a
fairly high temperature. And Scripture does indicate the first three days were
divided into light and darkness.

sound judgment, drawing one to a reasonable conclusion by weight of the overwhelming evidence.

Each of us places his faith in the view he *chooses* to accept, be it with God or without Him. Our choice is influenced by the system of morality we prefer. Men often select a morality with no absolutes, where there is no danger of punishment for evil deeds, rather than God's morality, with definite boundaries and consequences related to behavior.

> First of all, you must understand that in the last days scoffers will come, scoffing and following their own evil desires (II Pet. 3:3).

> Can you fathom the mysteries of God? Can you probe the limits of the Almighty? They are higher than the heavens — what can you do? They are deeper than the depths of the grave — what can you know? (Job 11:7-8).

CHAPTER SEVENTEEN

The Crowning Capstone of God's Creation: Man

"Haven't you read," he replied, "that at the beginning the Creator 'made them male and female'" (Matt. 19:4)?

For you created my inmost being; you knit me together in my mother's womb. I praise you because I am fearfully and wonderfully made; your works are wonderful, I know that full well (Psa. 139:13-14).

Genesis declares man to be the last of God's creations and the highest life form. Science agrees that man is the most complex and marvelous of all the species.

God is the Lover of Our Souls

Man is the most beautiful and perfect of all God's creations. God created man — with his intellect, his communication skills, his emotions, etc. — for a reason. He longs for a mutual, intimate relationship. The Song of Solomon reveals the infinite passion God has for mankind, not sexually, but romantically. God loves His creation. How sad it is that most often His love is not reciprocated.

A Wedding Present from God

The Earth, the sun, the moon and the stars — all were in preparation for the special relationship God had planned to have with mankind. Perhaps He sang as He carpeted the world with astoundingly beautiful meadows and lush vegetation — trees, ferns, flowers full of fragrance, plants of all shapes, color and design. Possibly He whistled cheerfully as He walled it with majestic mountains and canopied it with an awesome, starry sky. No doubt His heart was racing with expectancy as He called into being the mammals, the birds, the insects, the fish — all alive with amazing color, sound and motion. **(See fig. #93.)**

What was the excitement within the heart of God causing Him to burst forth with such creativity? It was the anticipation of a relationship with man — a creature still only in His imagination at that time.

Then, when all was ready, He created mankind — the epitome of what was beautiful and desirable to Him. Just what did this creature look like? — He looks like every son of Adam and she looks like every daughter of Eve.

God "Had a Ball"

God must have had a ball inventing the different characteristics for His creatures. Apparently he had never before seen anything like them; they were purely

Figure 93: A Wedding Present From God: Creation

products of His own creative imagination. He designed man last. From the dust, He began to fashion man with all his intricate parts: bones, as the framework of the body; muscles, which, when stimulated, contract and produce motion; various organs for specific functions in the body; glands, to remove materials from the blood and secrete them for further use in the body or for elimination; a voice box capable of making all sorts of sounds; and all the other parts — eyes, ears, nose, tongue, fingers, toes and so forth. **(See fig. #94.)**

Some people cannot conceive that God created pleasure. And yet many of man's features are not essential; they were simply put there for to be enjoyed. For instance, God gave man taste buds so he could take pleasure in eating. He gave man eyes to see in three-dimensional, living color.

Fashioned from the Dust

> Then God formed man of dust from the ground, and breathed into his nostrils the breath of life; and man became a living being (Gen. 2:7 NAS).

God fashioned man and all his magnificent characteristics. But something was still missing. Then God breathed the breath of life into man, and the "dust" became a living being. Suddenly, that dirt could speak, sing, paint, write, develop and play musical instruments, build computers, go to the moon, love, laugh, play, cry, whistle, do calculus, walk, run, jump, swim, think,

Figure 94: The Crowning Capstone of God's Creation: Man

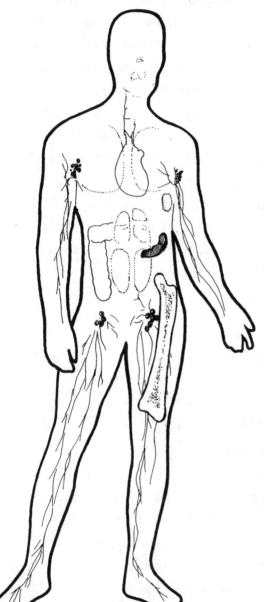

Brain:
   Computer

Eye: 3-D Color Motion
   Picture Camera

Ear:
   Stereo Sound System

Larynx:
   Speech Box

Lungs:
   Gas Exchange Plant

Heart:
   Pumping Station

Stomach & Intestines:
   Food Processing &
   Absorption Factory

Spleen:
   Defense System

Kidneys:
   Filtration Plant

Liver:
   Processing, Purification
   & Storage Factory

Hormones:
   Timekeeper & Messenger

Nervous System:
   Communication
   Network

Circulatory System:
   Transportation Network

Sex Organs:
   Reproduction Plant

Touch:
   Sensory Plant

imagine, invent, create, dream, worship, adore, praise. …
That was quite a breath God breathed into that dust!

Atheistic scientists have spent fortunes trying to
disprove Genesis 2:7, but they have not been able to find
any ingredient in man's body which is not also in dust.

Satan's Strategy

Satan will do anything he can to wound people so
they will not be able to receive the advances of God. He
knows that we humans tend to project the image of our
earthly fathers onto God, so he works to give children an
unhealthy view of their heavenly Father.

One of the greatest hindrances to romantic love
happens when one of the partners has no sense of his
own attractiveness. The devil tries to make us believe God
could never find us attractive. He constantly attacks our
self-image so that we will fail to recognize how beautiful
we are in God's eyes.

God continually holds out His hand to a people
who do not know Him. He is always there, anticipating
intimate fellowship with man, but rarely do we respond
to Him. Even many Christians scarcely know what it is to
have intimate fellowship with their heavenly Father. Some
change the tone of their voice in prayer or speak at an
abnormal pace, thinking it is intimate fellowship, when
often it is only a religious pretense. We do not do this with
those with whom we are in an intimate love relationship;
we only do this with those we do not know.

We Are the Beautiful Handiwork of God

Just how beautiful and special are we? There has never been a person like you before and there will never be another. Each and every person is totally unique — one of a kind. What makes a "one of a kind" in art, dress or sculpture so valuable and desirable? Its value is in being the only one of its kind in the entire universe.

Every person has the potential of revealing aspects of Jesus' personality and character never revealed or seen on this planet before, and which never will be seen except through that unique individual. So when we see an arrogant atheist who utters blasphemous curses at our God, or a bedraggled skid row bum, or a totally depraved transvestite — we realize he is a fallen human being who has the potential of revealing Jesus in a way no other being can or ever will — if he will become a vessel of honor. This is true of every person — no matter what his race, nationality or culture.

When we were conceived biologically, no matter what the circumstances were (rape, unwanted, etc.), — God began desiring a relationship with us from that first day. Each of us has the potential of bringing God incredible pleasure.

Misconceptions of God's Love

Our misconceptions of God's love often come as a result of our projecting onto God the inadequacies of our earthly father's love. God's love toward man has never ceased, even though man frequently does not respond to it.

But isn't mankind fallen, sinful — meaning our sins have separated us from God? How can we enter into close fellowship with such a holy and righteous God?

If my sweetheart wife fell into a slimy, stinky mud hole, would I divorce her — or would I labor to clean her up? If for some strange reason (with no rational justification at all) she returned to the mud, what would I do if I truly loved her? God considers us too valuable to give up on us, even when we are covered with mud. He makes an unceasing effort to clean us up and to get us to develop a hatred for mud (sin).

Some suggest God was a God of wrath and vengeance in the Old Testament until Christ came and died. Because of this misconception, man came up with the notion that God's wrath could be appeased by gifts, sacrifices, even blood and human sacrifices — or at least by suffering. Thus, man has attempted to worship God out of fear. Man has abused himself with rituals of torment in his self-efforts to become worthy to relate with God and experience His love. However, the *love* of God did not need to be restored (propitiation), because it was never lost. The death of Christ was to satisfy a legal requirement, to satisfy the just nature of God (Rom. 3:25, 26). The blood in the atonement signifies a cleansing agent, not a peace offering to an angry God. Christ died to declare His righteousness meets the requirement — to declare that God's justice and mercy are in perfect balance. If Christ hadn't died, thus leaving man to receive his due punishment, God's righteousness would not have been revealed — that He is a God of love and compassion as well as a God of justice.

When the Bible speaks of the wrath of God, it always is in reference to sin and unrighteousness, which are the objects of God's wrath (not man). This hatred will never be appeased or changed. Christ's death did not abate the righteous wrath of God toward sin; the universe could not survive if God should cease to hate sin. Nor did it increase God's love toward mankind, as some believe. God has always loved man with an all-consuming love. Nothing has ever, nor will ever, change that love.

God's Passion for His Bride Is Unabated

God's ultimate objective in the atonement was not to rescue souls from hell (that's a bonus), but to restore the ruptured relationship between Himself and His creation. God hates sin, but He loves every atheist, humanist, evolutionist, every murderer, thief, adulterer, homosexual — no matter how evil and sinful he is. He is patiently pursuing each sinner every day, all day long in hopes that man will turn from death to life. God finds no pleasure in the death of the wicked.

Jesus came to Earth "... to seek and to save what was lost" (Luke 19:10). What was lost? — The intimate, God-man relationship. The plan of redemption embraces everyone who does not know his Creator. All that is necessary is to acknowledge Him, repent of rebellion and sin, and make a commitment to follow, serve and obey Jesus, forever.

> For God did not send his Son into the world to condemn the world, but to save the world through him (Jn. 3:17).

CHAPTER EIGHTEEN

The Universe's Triune Testimony

To a Triune Creator God

Therefore go and make disciples of all nations, baptizing them in the name of the Father and of the Son and of the Holy Spirit (Matt. 28:19).

The Trinity

For most Christians, the Trinity is one of the most sophisticated, difficult and abstract topics of theology. They find it exceedingly difficult to connect the Trinity to practical issues in life. The Trinity is what distinguishes Christianity from all other religions.

Probably the most disturbing and most unsettling teaching in the entire Bible is that Jesus Christ, the son of a simple carpenter from a little town in Israel, was, in reality, God in human flesh. It was, and is, hard to think that God Himself came to mankind some 2,000 years ago and lived incognito, concealing Himself in human form.

"Son of God," when applied to Jesus, means God in the flesh. Christian theology attempts to define the being of God with three affirmations:

1) There is one God.

2) God exists in three persons.

3) The three persons are the Father, the Son and the Holy Spirit.

All evangelical Christians believe the above statement and that these three — though distinct — persons are only one God. However, to some it may seem to be a contradiction to speak of three persons in one God.

Some would argue the validity of the Trinity by saying it is ridiculous to maintain that $1 + 1 + 1 = 1$. It is said to be unscientific and foolish to assume God could be both one person and three personalities at the same time. Skeptics conclude, therefore, that Jesus wasn't God. That is, if God, in reality, actually exists.

The Trinity is not set forth in the Bible as an explicit doctrine, but is indirectly identified as Jesus speaks of Himself and of the Father and of the Holy Spirit. Scripture always presents the order of the Trinity with God the Father first, as the unseen source and Creator of all things. God, the Son, is second, tangibly and visibly revealing the Father to men and executing the will of God. God the Holy Spirit, is third, unseen yet revealing God the Son to men through the Word of God and through Spirit-filled believers. This order in Scripture is not an order of importance nor length of existence, for each member of the Godhead is equally eternal and equally God.

Three Ways to Experience God

Christian Schwarz in his book, *The Threefold Art of Experiencing God*, has provided an excellent understanding of the Christian doctrine or the Trinity. The following is a partial summary, which provides a practical understanding of the Trinity.

Creation theology reveals that the Trinitarian Godhead can be experienced in a three-fold way. The point here is not does one believe in the Trinity, but rather does one believe in a Trinitarian way. Just as light passing through a glass prism can be seen as different colors, so one can perceive God in various way. God is not simply a notion or a power. He is a person and the way God is known is in a relationship. There are three ways one can experience God, but if any one of the dimensions of God is neglected, the experiencing of God is incomplete.

The first expression of God is through creation. God revealed Himself as Creator by leaving marks of His handwriting on creation (Psa. 19:2; Rom. 1:19). This is revelation through creation.

The revelation of God through His Son illuminates God's plan of salvation. Here we see a different side of God and His character, gaining the understanding that Creator God has become fully man and yet still remains fully God (Col. 2:9). It is through this man, Jesus the Christ, that all mankind can be reconciled to God (II Cor. 5:19) and saved from eternal separation — the result of our sin and rebellion against the Creator. It is only a relationship with

Jesus Christ that will determine whether we experience salvation or eternal separation (Acts 4:12; Rom. 6:23).

Not only is there revelation of our God through creation and revelation of God through the Son, Jesus, but there is revelation of God through the third person of the Trinity, the Holy Spirit — God in us. Once we experience the truth of this revelation of God through salvation by the Son, God becomes a living reality within each Christian child of the living God.

God in Christ now lives within us (Gal. 2:20; 4:19; Col. 1:27). Thus, we enter into a new relationship with God as His Spirit enters into relationship with our spirit and we become "the temple of the Holy Spirit" (I Cor. 6:19).

The purpose of each way in which God reveals Himself is always aiming to establish a relationship with man. In each of the three revelations we encounter the one true God, but each time we encounter Him in a different way. This is revealed in the Bible. Whenever one of the three dimensions is neglected, there is an incomplete revelation and experience of God. It is obvious that the problems in the world result from an incomplete understanding of the three-fold revelation of God.

Each person of the Trinity has a particular dimension and purpose for fulfilling the work of God in an individual's life. The Father is to reveal the work of the Creator in and through creation, while the Son is to reveal the work of God in and through salvation and the Holy Spirit is to reveal the work of God in and through sanctification. Each member of the Trinity reveals, not only the work of God, but also the places or ways God meets with us. God the Father meets externally on the outside of us in creation. The Son meets alongside us or among us in salvation and the Holy Spirit meets within us providing insight into His revelations.

Each member of the Trinity addresses us in three different ways. The Father appeals to our minds through creation, the Son appeals to our heart through the salvation invitation and the Holy Spirit appeals to our spirit by empowering us. Those who have come to know God in all three ways will be able to fulfill God's divine plan and destiny for his or her life.[xxv]

The Universe is Fundamentally a Trinity of Trinities

There seems to be a basic system of three-in-oneness pervading the entire creation, clearly reflecting the triune relationship in the entire physical universe. The doctrine of the Trinity is not only sound mathematically, but is reflected in all true science in an incredible way. The concept of an existing triune God is essential for the universe to be meaningfully understood and explained. While the following examples do not actually prove the Creator's existence or His triune being, it certainly is difficult to arrive at any other satisfactory explanation for the reason of such a universal trinity in nature.

Space, Matter and Time

The reality of the triune nature of the Creator is

evident in creation, which is clearly a tri-universe composed of space, matter and time. It is further remarkable that each of these three entities is also a trinity. **(See fig. #95.)**

Scientists tell us that space consists of exactly three dimensions: Length, width and depth — each of which is equally important and absolutely necessary in order for space to be reality. There would be no space, if there were only two dimensions instead of three. Thus, while there are three distinct dimensions each contains the whole of space. In order to calculate the amount of any given part of space, one does not add the length and width and depth, but rather multiplies them together. Similarly, the mathematics of the Trinity is not $1 + 1 + 1 = 1$, rather it is $1 \times 1 \times 1 = 1$.

Matter **(see fig. #96)** comprises another part of the universe, and its nature provides an even more remarkable analogy with the Trinity. Matter involves these three facets: Energy, motion and phenomenon; there is nothing that exists which cannot directly be included in one of these. Each part of matter is distinct, yet each involves the whole of matter and none of the three parts can exist by itself without the other two. It is interesting that energy is first in order, but this is not an arrangement of importance. Motion, which reveals energy, is second part and it is produced by energy. Phenomenon comes from motion and makes up or comprises the ways in which motion is revealed to man. Even so, the Holy Spirit

Figure 95: Space and the Trinity

Space consists of three dimensions: length, width and depth. To calculate space, one does not add the length, width and depth, but multiplies them. Similarly, the mathematics of the Trinity is not 1 + 1 + 1 = 3, but 1 x 1 x 1 = 1.

reveals the Son, and through Him the Father is revealed to man.

Lastly, we find time as the third entity, consisting of the future, the present and the past. **(See fig. #97.)** Each part of time contains the entire aspect of time; it is distinct, and yet each entity cannot exist without the other two. The future is the unseen element of time and is embodied and made real, moment by moment, in the present. The past comes out from the present, becomes invisible and yet continually influences us.

Figure 96: Matter and the Trinity

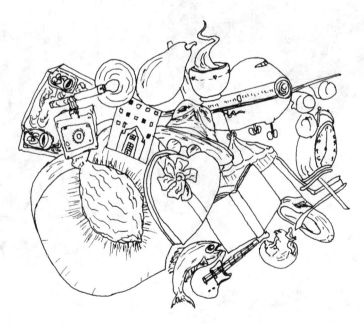

Matter, another part of the universe, also is a trinity: energy, motion and phenomenon.

Figure 97: Space and the Trinity

Time comprises the third and final part of the universe; like matter and space, it is comprised of a trinity: past, present and future.

We see that the universe consists of space, is made visible in matter, and is experienced or affected through time. Each one of these three entities is distinct and yet makes up the entire aspect of creation. It is amazing to see how every detail of the physical universe remarkably parallels biblical revelation of the Trinity. This cannot be coincidence. There must be a sufficient and meaningful cause for these agreements. It is therefore not at all unreasonable, but rather exceedingly realistic, to believe that the Bible reveals that a triune God is the Creator of the tri-universe.

Man, a Tri-Part Being: Body, Soul and Spirit

> May God himself, the God of peace, sanctify you through and through. May your whole spirit, soul and body be kept blameless at the coming of our Lord Jesus Christ (I Thes. 5:23).

Trinity is Imperative

The significance of the Trinity is this: If there is no Trinity, God is not love; and there could be no love, because love only exists in the context of relationships. Understanding the intrinsic value of the Trinity is absolutely essential, for if the Trinity has not always existed, then God's nature cannot be that of love. If one could go back far enough in time, the point would eventually be reached when no created being was yet in existence. If God was alone at this time, without even

the other two members of the Trinity, then there could
have been no love, for love only exists in the context
of relationships. But since God has always been three-
in-one, He was never really alone and love was always
present among the members of the Trinity.

Satan, knowing full well the significance of the Trinity,
seeks to destroy this truth. Every cult, including the
Mormons, the Jehovah's Witnesses and Islam (a spin-off
of Christianity), as well as New Age cults, will deny the
existence of the Trinity. The doctrine of the Trinity is an
indispensable truth; for if there is no Trinity, there is no
love. Love only exists in the context of relationships.

God in Christ

Non-Christians who do not have a theological
background are often confused by statements such as,
"the Son of God was sent to be God's provision for sin"
or "the second person of the Trinity became the sacrifice
for sin." So it cannot be emphasized enough that it was
God Himself in Jesus of Nazareth who came to redeem
us. It was not merely the second member of a triad of
individuals who made a personal visit to Earth, because
" ... God was in Christ reconciling the world to Himself
..." (II Cor. 5:19 NAS). When we become Christians we do
not enter into three relationships. We enter into a single
relationship with one God Who is known to us as Father,
Who was present in Christ and Who was made real to us
by the Spirit.

The doctrine of the Trinity is no primitive, unscientific absurdity, rather it relates intensely to everyday reality. Recently, it has been observed in physics that the identities of two atomic particles can disappear and their properties merge; yet they remain two individual particles. This is a perfect representation of how God was manifested and revealed by and in His Son, Who as a man was Jesus Christ and yet is one with the Father.

Let us use this metaphor: In the drama of redemption, there are three roles. But the three roles are played by two rather than three actors. The role of judge is played by God. The role of the accused is played by man. The role of substitute or Savior is played again by God — not by some third actor.

The Doctrine of Substitution

When we try to understand the New Testament doctrine of substitution, we must bear in mind the close unity between God the Judge and Christ the Savior. In the process of salvation, God is not transferring the penalty from one man who is guilty to another who is innocent; God is bearing the penalty Himself. J. B. Phillips states it masterfully in "Good News" (173-174):

> Now if the lonely figure hanging on the cross so long ago were merely a great and good man, martyred for his beliefs, then that is regrettable, but hardly of any significance to us today. But if it was God who was murdered, if it was God who willingly allowed the forces of evil to close in upon

Him and kill Him, then we are in the presence of something which, though it happened in time, is of eternal significance. We are looking upon something utterly foreign to any other religion. We are seeing God allowing Himself not only to be personally involved in the folly, sin and downright evil of the human situation, but accepting death at the hands of His own creatures.

This is unknown to the majority of people. We must use every skill of communication, every device of writer, artist, poet and dramatist to break the insulation of ignorance and let men see Who died upon the cross. (See fig. #98.)

The crucifixion of God is an incalculable mystery. It goes so far beyond the ordinary man's ideas of God, sin, forgiveness and reconciliation, that the mind is carried out of its depth and the heart is overwhelmed by the dreadful significance of the event. Once people begin to realize that the man on the cross was no demigod, no puppet-godling, no fragmented piece of the Godhead, but God Himself, there is bound to be an explosion in their thinking.

Once we have seen the vision of the crucified God, we begin to see the light that penetrates the darkness of human suffering. The Bible knows no dualism of personality or attitude in God. He who has seen Jesus has seen the God of the Old Testament as well. The Word has always been with God and has also always been God. The

Figure 98: "Who Died on the Cross?"

only change from Old to New Testaments is that the Word became flesh, and Jesus revealed the heart of God.

There can be nothing more important for any individual than to become rightly related to this tri-universe and its triune God. Of course, this means unreserved acceptance of Christ as Lord and Savior.

For in Christ all the fullness of the Deity lives in bodily form (Col. 2:9).

> "The virgin will be with child and will give birth to a son, and they will call him Immanuel" — which means "God with us" (Matt. 1:23).

> In the beginning was the Word, and the Word was with God, and the Word was God. He was with God in the beginning. Through him all things were made; without him nothing was made that has been made (John 1:1-3).

Conclusion

This book, in its attempt to destroy the myth of evolutionism, may appear to be overkill; however, I find it enjoyable to demolish the enemy's camp. Our enemy is not flesh and blood, but rather the age-old dragon who has become a useful idiot in the hands of God.

The conclusion, then, is obvious to one willing to discover the truth. The evidence of incredible design is everywhere.

> The heavens declare the glory of God; the skies proclaim the work of his hands (Psa. 19:1).

> For since the creation of the world God's invisible qualities — his eternal power and divine nature — have been clearly seen, being understood from what has been made, so that men are without excuse (Rom. 1:20).

Natural selection proposed by Darwin was supposed to get rid of design and purpose, by teaching that life and living organisms were the results of blind accidents.

Three Distinct Arguments in Favor of a Creator

1) The Cosmological Argument: A Creator Force

Whenever something exists, there must be an external cause behind its existence. Whatever is the cause, must ultimately be non-contingent, uncaused by anything else, totally self-reliant, powerful, eternal, etc. We call the cause God. This argument is why most mathematicians and astronomers believe in a Creator God.

2) The Teleological Argument: An Intelligent Force

Our world and universe are designed for a purpose (Isa. 45:18). The human body with its amazing complexity is a proof of a Creator (Psa. 8). There is an intelligent force behind the creation of everyone.

3) The Moral Argument: A Moral Force

All human beings are created in the image of God and have a sense of right and wrong. When we are in sin, we have a tendency to deny the reality of God. Why does the world rise up against atrocities? The animal kingdom doesn't. They do not feel remorse. Why do we have a sense of accountability to one another and their property?

The Bible declares without apology that, "men are without excuse." Think what that means. No one will ever be able to stand before God and tell Him there is a good excuse for not believing in and obeying the call of God. Every human who ever lived has had the clear evidence of the designs and intricacies of creation loudly declared to them — there is an Almighty God Who made all of creation. His Name is Jesus, and He desires to have a personal relationship with each and every person on planet Earth.

> But whoever drinks the water I give him will never thirst. Indeed, the water I give him will become

in him a spring of water welling up to eternal life
(John 4:14).

The Creator's Plan for Mankind: Blessings Forevermore

The theme of blessing is especially prominent in the
Book of Genesis. The book opens with God's blessing
of all creatures, particularly humans (Gen. 1) and ends
with Jacob blessing his sons in Egypt (Gen. 49). The full
application of God's promises and the extension of His
blessing is a hope of better things in the future. The saints
in the Old Testament, as well as those since the coming
of Jesus, have lived with the hope of a new age in which
there will be no more pain and anguish and in which the
goodness of God will embrace them forevermore. This
expectation of a new state of harmonious and blessed
existence is referred to as "the city of God" in the Book of
Hebrews:

> For he [Abraham] was looking forward to the city
> with foundations, whose architect and builder is
> God (Heb. 11:10).

> For here we do not have an enduring city, but we are
> looking for the city that is to come (Heb. 13:14).

The title of this book is *The Origin Controversy:
Creation by Design or Chance.* It goes without saying, the
evidence is overwhelmingly in favor of Creation by design.

Endnotes

[i] Biology Textbook qtd. by John W. Heffner in Evidence for Creation Seminar. DVD.

[ii] ibid.

[iii] Horgan, J. "The New Social Darwinists." *Scientific American* 273. Oct 1995.

[iv] Bozarth, Richard. "The Meaning of Evolutionism." *American Atheist.* Feb 1978:30.

[v] Johnson, Philip E. "The Unraveling of Scientific Materialism." *First Things 77.* November 1997:22.

[vi] Maddox, John. "Down with the Big Bang." *NATURE* 34 August 1989.

[vii] Hoyle, Fred. "The Big Bang Under Attack." *SCIENCE DIGEST* 92 May 1984: 84.

[viii] "Have Astronauts Found God?" *Reader's Digest.* July 1980.

[ix] Corey, M. A. *God and the New Cosmology: The Anthropic Design Argument.* Lanham, Md.: Rowman & Littlefield, 1993. 135.

[x] *National Geographic.* May, 1974: 625.

[xi] Colson, Chuck. *How Now Shall We Then Live?* 63.

[xii] Sullivan, J. W. N. *The Limitation of Science.*

[xiii] Watson, D. M. S. *Nature* 1929: 233.

[xiv] *Witchita Eagle-Beacon* 24 Feb. 1989.

[xv] "Scientist Tunes in to Gene Compositions." *San Jose Mercury News.* 13 May 1986 as qtd. in *Science Frontiers Online.* No. 46: July/August 1986. http://www.science-frontiers.com/sf046p08.htm

[xvi] Angrist, Stanley. "Perpetual Motion Machines." *Scientific American* Jan. 1968: 115-122.

[xvii] Huxley, Julian. *Evolutionism in Action.* 1953.

[xviii] *Unlocking The Mystery Of Life.* Videocassette. Focus on the Family, 2002.

[xix] Kerri & Kimmi. "Intelligent Design." http://www.creationinthecrossfire.com/articles/twintopics1.html.

[xx] Davies, Paul C. *The Accidental Universe.* Cambridge: Cambridge University Press, 1982. 90.

[xxi] Joseph, Michael. *The Intelligent Universe.* London, 1983:256. as qtd. by Oller Jr., John W. "Not According to Hoyle." Univ. of N. Mexico.

[xxii] Siegfried, Tom. "The Incredible Lightness of Being." *The Dallas Morning News* 19 Oct. 2003: H1+

[xxiii] "Anthropic Reasoning." *Kavli-CERCA Cosmology Conference.* Case Western Reserve University, Dept. of Physics. 11 October 2003. http://www.phys.cwru.edu/events_cerca_video_archive.php.

[xxiv] "Is Man Back In The Center?" *Science Digest August* 1986.

[xxv] Schwarz, Christian A. *The Threefold Art of Experiencing God.* Carol Sream, Il.: ChurchSmart Resources, 1999.

BIBLIOGRAPHY

Non-Christian Books

*Funk & Wagnalls Standard Dictionary of Folklore,
Mythology, and Legend.* Ed. Maria Leach. San
Francisco, California: Harper & Row Publishers,
1972.

Christian Books

Bliss, Richard B. *Origins: Creation or Evolution.* El Cajon,
California: Creation-Life Publishers Inc., 1988.

Blocher, Henri. *In the Beginning.* Leicester, England:
Inter-Varsity Press, 1984.

Clark, Harold W. *The Battle Over Genesis.* Washington,
D.C.: Review and Herald Publishing Association,
1977.

Coffin, Harold G. *Creation — Accident or Design?*
Washington, D.C.: Review and   Herald
Publishing Association, 1969.

Colson, Charles and Nancy Pearcey. *How Now Shall We
Then Live?* Wheatland, Il.: Tyndale, 1999.

Corey, M. A. *God and the New Cosmlogy: The Anthropic*

Design Argument. Lanham, Md.: Rowman & littlefield, 1993. 135.

Criswell, W. A. *Did Man Just Happen?* Grand Rapids, Michigan: Zondervan Publishing House, 1957.

Dillow, Joseph C. *The Waters Above: Earth's Pre-Flood Vapor Canopy.* Chicago: Moody Press, 1981.

Epp, Theodore H. *The God of Creation.* Lincoln, Nebraska: Back to the Bible, 1972.

Gamlin, Linda. *Evolutionism.* Eyewitness Science. Toronto, Canada: Stoddart Publishing Co., Limited, 1993.

Geisler, Norman L. and J. Kerby Anderson. *Origin Science: A Proposal for the Creation-Evolution Controversy.* Grand Rapids, Michigan: Baker Book House, 1987.

Gish, Duane T. *The Amazing Story of Creation from Science and the Bible.* El Cajon, California: Institute for Creation Research, 1990.

Haum, Charles A. *Genesis: Chapters One Through Five.* Goldsboro, North Carolina: Teaching All Nations Publishers, 1984.

Hill, Harold. *From God to You by Way of the Zoo.* Old Tappan, New Jersey: Fleming H. Revell Company, 1985.

Kester, Phyllis. *What's All This Monkey Business?* Harrison, Arkansas: New Leaf Press, 1981.

Kofahl, Robert E. and Kelly L. Segraves. *The Creation Explanation.* San Diego, California: Creation-Science Research Center, 1975.

McLean, Dr. G. S., Roger Oakland and Larry McLean. *The Evidence For Creation.* Canada: Full Gospel Bible Institute, 1989.

Morris, Henry M. *The Beginning of the World.* Denver, Colorado: Accent Books, 1977.

Morris, Henry M. *Biblical Cosmology and Modern Science.* Nutley, New Jersey: Craig Press, 1970.

Morris, Henry M. *The Genesis Record.* Grand Rapids, Michigan: Baker Book House, 1976.

Morris, Henry M. *King of Creation.* San Diego, California: CLP Publishers, 1980.

Morris, Henry M. *The Remarkable Birth of Planet Earth.* San Diego, California: Institute for Creation Research, 1972.

Morris, Henry M. *Scientific Creationism.* San Diego, California: Creation-Life Publishers, 1974.

Morris, Henry M. *Studies in the Bible and Science.* Philadelphia, Pennsylvania: Presbyterian and

Reformed Publishing Co., 1966.

Morris, Henry M. *The Troubled Waters of Evolution.* San Diego, California: Creation- Life Publishers, 1974.

Morris, Henry M. and Gary E. Parker. *What is Creation Science?* San Diego, California: Creation-Life Publishers, 1982.

Newman, Robert C. and Herman J. Eckelmann, Jr. *Genesis One and the Origin of the Earth.* Grand Rapids, Michigan: Baker Book House, 1981.

Petersen, Dennis R. *Unlocking the Mystery of Creation.* El Cajon, California: Master Books, 1987.

Ramm, Bernard. *The Christian View of Science and Scripture.* Grand Rapids, Michigan: William B. Eerdman's Publishing Co., 1954.

Rehwinkel, Alfred M. *The Wonders of Creation.* Grand Rapids, Michigan: Baker Book House, 1974.

Richards, Lawrence. *It Couldn't Just Happen.* Fort Worth, Texas: Sweet Publishing, 1987.

Schaeffer, Francis A. *No Final Conflict.* Downers Grove, Illinois: Inter-Varsity Press, 1975.

Segraves, Kelly L. *The Way It Was.* San Diego, California: Beta Books, 1976.

Schwarz, Christian A. *The Threefold Art of Experiencing God.* Carol Stream, Illinois: ChurchSmart Resources, 1999.

Wiester, John. *The Genesis Connection.* New York: Thomas Nelson Publishers, 1983.

Wilder-Smith, A. E. *The Creation of Life.* San Diego, California: Master Books, 1970.

Wilder-Smith, A. E. *Man's Origin, Man's Destiny.* Minneapolis, Minnesota: Bethany Fellowship, Inc., 1975.

Wilder-Smith, A. E. *The Natural Sciences Know Nothing of Evolution.* San Diego, California: Master Books, 1981.

Video

Unlocking The Mystery Of Life. Videocassette. Focus on the Family, 2002.

List of Graphs & Illustrations

1. Atlas Balancing the Earth on His Shoulders

2. An Ancient Concept of the Earth's Composition

3. A Hindu Belief Regarding the Way the Earth Is Held

4. Which Came First, the Chicken or the Egg?

5. Ptolemy's Conception of an Earth-Centered Universe

6. The Evolutionary Concept of How a Solar System Is Formed

7. The Big Bang Theory (Cosmic Egg Theory)

8. Mt. St. Helens after the 1980 Eruption

9. Abnormalities within Our Solar System

10. Building Blocks of Creation

11. Building Materials for Construction

12. Building Blocks for the Construction of an Atom

13. God Created in Steps

14. "Let There Be Light"

15. The Incredible Atom

16. The Desolate Moon

17. Water — There Is Nothing Like It

18. The Water Molecule Will Not Combine With Other Molecules

19. The Bond Angle of a Water Molecule

20. Boiling and Freezing Characteristics of Water

(Footnotes)

[1]   The second law of thermodynamics is discussed in Volume II and is also discussed in chapter ten of this volume.

[2]   All the electromagnetic force systems (all types of energy except gravity and the nuclear forces) are essentially different forms of light energy operating at different wave lengths. Even the nuclear forces involve the velocity of light.

[3]   The spring of Gihon is another water place where God can be seen in action (Gen 2:3; I Ki.1:33, 38, 45; II Chron. 32:30; 33:14).

[4]   The Gap Theory concept is covered in volume 7 of the Creation Science series and chapter 16 of this book .

[5]   The young Earth concept is covered in volumes 8 and 9 of the Creation Science series.

[6]   Scientifically, there is always light — measurable electromagnetic radiation (light wave) — wherever there is any matter at all at a temperature above absolute zero, but such radiation is usually not visible unless the matter is at a fairly high temperature. And Scripture does indicate the first three days were divided into light and darkness.

(Endnotes)